THE Three Commas Club

A True Story of Sex Trafficking Pedophilia & Murder

Jack Watts

The only thing necessary
For evil to triumph
Is for good men to do nothing.

–Edmund Burke

Copyright © 2020 by John T. (Jack) Watts

Published by Five Moon Press, Atlanta, Georgia

All rights reserved. No part of this book may be reproduced in any form or by any means, electronic, or mechanical, including photocopying, or by any information storage or retrieval system. Written permission must be secured from the publisher to use or reproduce any part of this book—except for brief quotations in critical reviews or articles.

ISBN: 978-1-5136-7574-9

Printed in The United States of America

Contents

Introduction 9
1 Don't Come, There's an Emergency 13
2 An Enigma Wrapped in a Conundrum 29
3 He Did Cross the Line 47
4 The Dam Had Broken 59
5 Break Her Longstanding Silence 73
6 He Had a Large Carving Knife 91
7 No Evidence of Disease 97
8 Fishing Without a License 107
9 A Heart Over the "I" 115
10 A Solid Grip on Her Rear 125
11 The Rarely Traveled Road 135
12 He Would Eventually Go to Jail 143
13 Her Year from Hell 155
14 Dead in Twenty Minutes 169
15 Terrifying People 181
16 Apprehension about the FBI 191
17 It Could Cost You Your Life 199
18 A Herculean Task 209
19 Trumpet the Rights of the Innocent 219
20 Back in the Game 227
21 A Strategic Decision 239
Conclusion 247

The Three Commas Club
A True Story of Sex Trafficking, Pedophilia and Murder

Introduction

Hi, my name is Jack Watts. I am the author of a couple dozen books. I am also very active on social media. Because of these two things, people frequently approach me asking, "Would you write my story? If you do, I know it would be a best seller and we would make millions."

I cannot tell you how many times I've heard this or something similar. In the case of Emily Chamber's story, however, it might be true. What she divulged to me might even become headline news. It's a distinct possibility.

What you are about to read is a true story—not just parts of it but all of it. No aspect of The Three Commas Club has been fabricated or embellished, not even a little. People often say truth is stranger than fiction. In the case of The Three Commas Club, this is absolutely accurate.

Because this story is so powerful and shocking, it is an absolute necessity for me to protect the innocent. Therefore, for Emily's safety and my personal protection, I have changed the names and places in the book—all of them. My name is the only one that is accurate. Being the author, there was no way for me to conceal my identity. This definitely increases my vulnerability, but I had no choice other than to expose myself and move forward, leaving my safety in the hands of God.

Despite this not being my story, I have become a key player in it. This was not by choice. Because of events beyond the control of either Emily or me, my role has become much more than that of a passive writer. In fact, as the story has developed, I became the driving force behind uncovering a pattern of criminality that has flourished in plain sight by some of America's most powerful and financially affluent people. What they have done has been happening with impunity for decades.

By writing this story about sex trafficking, pedophilia and even murder, I have vicariously shared in Emily's travails. Because of my actions, I have knowingly and willingly put myself in harm's way. I have placed myself in the crosshairs of several powerful, evil men. By bringing their exploitations to light by writing *The Three Commas Club*, I have knowingly put both Emily's life and mine on the line. I have done this hoping that by exposing decades of criminal behavior to the light of day, I might help future victims avoid the degrading fate of being sexually exploited.

The Three Commas Club is different than any book I have ever written. Like many of my earlier works, it is a true story. The difference between this book and those that preceded it is this book has been written in real time.

When I began, I had no idea how it would end or even if it would conclude at all. I doubted there would be a Perry Mason moment bringing everything together for a happy conclusion. Real life isn't like that.

Instead, I suspected events beyond my control would determine what the ending would be. Although neither Emily nor I knew what the future would hold, we did know this story required being told. At least, this is how we both felt in the beginning.

Because *The Three Commas Club* involves actual events that occurred nearly fifteen years ago and most likely are continuing to this day, there is an element of risk that is being taken by me to make this story available to readers like you.

Because there is no way to accept or mitigate what has transpired, nor justify such aberrant behavior in any way, I have been compelled to write this book. As I perceived my role, once I was completely aware of the level of depravity that was being championed by the members of The Three Commas Club, I didn't have any other option—not and maintain my personal sense of self-worth or my Christian values.

What the future will hold by stepping out boldly as I have is anybody's guess—*que sera, sera*. I'm moderately apprehensive. Emily is scared to death, terrified actually. When you read *The Three Commas Club*, you will understand why she feels this way. Her fears and apprehensions are justified, so are mine.

If you think any of my previous books have been page turners, you haven't seen anything yet. *The Three Commas Club* is about to knock your socks off. I assure you it will.

Just one more thing. You'll notice this book does not contain a Preface. This leaves me no place to name those who have helped me along the way. I have done this on purpose to provide anonymity to those who have provided me with insight, guidance and encouragement along the way. In this unique case, by not naming them, I have done them a favor.

Nevertheless, I know who you are, and I am deeply grateful for your contributions.

Now, without further ado, let's begin.

THE THREE COMMAS CLUB

CHAPTER 1

Don't Come, There's an Emergency

NOVEMBER 11, 2004

"I'm sorry, Mrs. Chambers, I would love to help you but I can't. Both of Saturday's flights to Saint Thomas are completely booked." Taking a deep breath, the Delta ticket agent added, "My advice is for you to keep the ticket you already have. If you don't, looking at the schedule, it will be Tuesday before the next seat is available."

Hearing this, Emily Chambers wasn't surprised but the news distressed her nonetheless. Being the second week in November, shortly after the traditional beginning of the vacation season in the U.S. Virgin Island—or any Caribbean island for that matter—there were rarely any empty seats on either of the two direct flights from Nashville headed for Cyril E. King Airport in Charlotte Amalie, Saint Thomas, Virgin Islands.

Emily had to arrive on the island no later than Saturday. There was no question about that. Her job depended on it. Despite being required to do so, her husband had expressly forbidden her to arrive that Friday as she had originally planned.

His insistence that she change her flight placed her in an impossible situation. There was no way for her to win—not and comply with her husband's firm demand. She certainly didn't want to defy him. Doing so wasn't an option. Having been married to James "Bruiser" Chambers for a decade, she knew better than to disobey him. There would be a terrible price to pay if she did.

He had been perfectly clear about what he wanted. In no uncertain terms, he had commanded. "Don't come Friday! There's an emergency." He didn't elaborate about what the nature of the emergency was either. He would never be that accommodating, not to his wife. What the cause of the emergency happened to be was his business and not hers. She understood this completely.

When he made a command, he expected Emily to comply, to do exactly what he told her without explanation, unnecessary questions or undesired deviations. It was as simple as that.

Through painful experience Emily had come to understand her husband always meant what he said. When he gave her a firm command like this one, it was clear he would not take kindly to being disobeyed. She had learned her lesson about going against him the hard way.

Emily's problem was she was scheduled to work at their newly opened restaurant, Fisherman's North Drop, on Saturday afternoon. If there had been a seat on Saturday morning's flight, she would be able to make it on time for work but this wasn't an option. The flight was already overbooked. This created a significant dilemma. She had to follow her husband's directive, but she couldn't be AWOL from fulfilling her responsibilities at the restaurant either.

Bruiser's boss and mentor, Daren Magnus, certainly wasn't a man to be crossed either. If she wasn't present at the restaurant by Saturday afternoon as she had been scheduled to be, Daren would take it out on both her husband and her. This would put her in trouble with two men and not just one. Hence her predicament.

Emily was in an impossible situation. Being damned if she did or damned if she didn't, she concluded that she had no alternative other than to stick with her original plan and fly to Saint Thomas the following morning. What else could she do? Besides, she was already packed and ready to go.

Surely Bruiser would understand her dilemma and not be cross with her. She tried to convince herself of this, but she could never be certain—not with him. His nature was extremely volatile, especially when she willfully disobeyed one of his clear directives.

. . .

Having made her decision to stick to her original plan, she arrived at Nashville International early Friday morning for the mandatory screening, which had been implemented shortly after the attack on the Twin Towers three years earlier. After eating a croissant with coffee, Emily boarded the crowded flight filled with vacationers who were all in much better spirits than she was. She envied them and wished her life was as trouble-free as most of theirs appeared to be.

Upon arrival in Saint Thomas nearly five hours later, a great adventure was about to await her fellow passengers, but Emily was uncertain about what would await her. Would her husband be reasonable or would he be furious that she hadn't been able to arrive on Saturday's flight as he had demanded? Would Bruiser understand she had no alternative other than to keep her seat or would he take out his anger on her for not being able to accomplish the impossible?

In her heart, she hoped he would be understanding, but she also knew this was probably nothing more than wishful thinking. That Delta had no seats available on the Saturday flight wouldn't matter to Bruiser. All that would matter to him was she had disobeyed his command.

It hadn't always been like this between them. In the beginning, Bruiser had been kind and gentle with her, but that was then, a long time ago. Over the years he had changed but certainly not for the better. Forsaking chivalry and his marital commitment to cherish her, he had become vicious and brutal, striking and kicking her routinely when she didn't do exactly what he demanded, in precisely the way he wanted it to be done. When he insisted upon something, regardless of what it was or how trivial it might be, she was not allowed to deviate from his directives, not one iota. When she did, there was always hell to pay. She had the physical and emotional scars to prove it.

She had thought about leaving him numerous times but always found a reason to stay or, more accurately, invented a reason to stay. This is the kind of mental gymnastics battered women experience, and Emily Chambers had certainly become a physically, psychologically and emotionally abused wife.

Not everything was difficult between them though. In fact, some things were quite good. Financially, they had become very successful, especially since Daren Magnus had become Bruiser's mentor several years earlier. Loving the affluence and the growth in their financial portfolio, all of which had occurred since Magnus had entered their lives, like so many abused women in America, Emily deceived herself into believing her husband's brutal tirades would eventually subside and the two of them would blissfully grow old together. In her magical thinking, she envisioned them enjoying the fruitful bounty affluence produced, retiring to a dream life of leisure.

Although she often escaped reality to enjoy her whimsical fancies, this was certainly not the way she felt that Friday morning. Having left a message on his cell phone that she was coming just before departing, when the plane landed in Charlotte Amalie, Emily was one of the first passengers to disembark. She hoped that, by not making her husband wait, this might help with his mood. This was her desire but certainly not her reality. Her wish that Bruiser would be understanding evaporated the moment she noticed the furious look on his face. Instantly seeing how livid he was, she nearly wet her pants.

She had not done what he had commanded. That she hadn't was all that mattered to him. She could see it on his face. Emily's explanation about why she had to come on Friday would fall on deaf ears. In this furious state, Bruiser was not interested in any of her flimsy excuses.

Retrieving her luggage from the carousel, he dragged her bags outside roughly, practically throwing them into the back of the white Toyota Forerunner that was parked out front. Because Bruiser was cursing loudly every step of the way, the travelers who passed by felt very uncomfortable. Wisely, the vacationers gave him a wide berth.

Bruiser didn't care that he was making a scene, quite the contrary. Having seen his hostile countenance many times before, Emily knew her husband actually hoped someone would challenge his belligerency. Being confrontational with a stranger might provide him with a much-needed outlet for his rage, but nobody was foolish enough to challenge him, not and risk an altercation with a formidable bully like Bruiser.

Tall and athletic, Bruiser was a 6'5", 250 pound, forty-year-old man with an impressive physique. Although he looked like a recently retired NFL linebacker, in his younger days Bruiser had actually played baseball and not football. This is where he got his nickname. Christened James, if one of his pitches hit a batter, which happened frequently, it would always create a bruise; hence the nickname. He used his wildness to his advantage.

Now that his short-lived baseball career was over and he had become a very successful businessman, he left everything about baseball behind except for his unique sobriquet. Being a bully, he loved being called Bruiser.

Emily understood the reason why. She was no novice where her husband's rages were concerned. Recognizing how near he was to crossing the line from verbal abuse to a physical altercation, she did not respond to anything Bruiser said or did on their short drive to Magnus's compound named Viol. It was located just a few miles from Cyril E. King International Airport.

Knowing better than to engage Bruiser along the way, she wisely kept her mouth shut and her eyes focused straight ahead. She knew from experience that being tranquil and stoic was her best defense.

Arriving, Bruiser turned into Estate Viol, which was surrounded by a majestic white six-foot concrete wall. Once there, Emily was relieved to finally get out of the SUV. She wanted to put as much distance between herself and her husband as possible, without actually running away from him. As angry as Bruiser had become, she wasn't convinced he wouldn't hit her, even with so many people being present at the estate. She didn't think he would but he was only inches away from exploding. That he was on the verge was something she understood well.

She counted on the hope that hitting her with others watching would make him look bad to Daren and this was something Bruiser would never intentionally do. Once out of the SUV, taking several strides away from the automobile, Emily stopped to look around.

Despite experiencing fear and dread, she couldn't help but love the view. Everything was so beautiful. Magnus's compound was truly magnificent. Daren had purchased it a few years earlier for $15 million, after the bull market had crashed in 2002. When this happened, the estate's owner needed cash quickly so he jumped at Daren's offer, despite the fact it was well below the estate's true market value.

The compound was quite large, but it didn't have a traditional house. Estates in the islands weren't built like that. Instead, it had a series of smaller buildings that surrounded a very large swimming pool in the center of the compound. The living area and master bedroom were in one building, which was separated from the kitchen, dining room, and several smaller bedrooms by a breezeway connecting the two central buildings.

The sprawling Magnus compound was tastefully appointed, immaculately kept and in pristine condition. Every aspect of it was inviting. There were bungalow suites on the estate as well. Each had a bedroom, bathroom, living room and small kitchenette. When the Chambers were in town, which they were required to be for half of the year for tax purposes, one of the bungalows was reserved for them.

Knowing where to go, carrying nothing in her hands other than her purse, Emily headed straight for their bungalow. She made certain to stay well ahead of her skulking husband. Walking into their bungalow, she expected Bruiser to follow with her luggage but this didn't happen. Instead, once she was in the bathroom to relieve herself after her long flight, she heard the door to the bungalow shut loudly.

This surprised her. Suspecting what it meant, she quickly finished. Then, she walked to the door but it wouldn't open. Just as she had feared, it had been locked from the outside. As bizarre as it might seem, the outside of the door had the lock on it, not the inside. Unlike any other place she had ever been, there was no lock on the inside of their bungalow door. Instead, the lock had been placed on the outside. All of the other bungalows on Estate Viol were just like this. It hadn't been done by mistake. This meant she had no way to keep anybody out, even during times of intimacy with her husband. They had absolutely no privacy whatsoever, if someone chose to enter. No one ever did, but the thought that it might happen always troubled her.

Because of this bizarre arrangement, she was imprisoned—trapped inside their bungalow with no way to escape. With the bungalow's windows being plexiglass and sealed, coupled with there being no second door to exit, she couldn't leave until her husband returned to open the door. With spotty phone service, she couldn't call for help either. Besides, she knew better than to even try. Such a betrayal would cost her dearly.

At first, perplexed by her situation, she just sat there, but this didn't last very long. Although just 5'3" and 112 pounds soaking wet, Emily may have been a battered wife, but she was certainly not a passive woman. At times as feisty as a bulldog, her fear of Bruiser quickly turned to anger. That he would have the audacity to lock her up was infuriating. Emily wondered what kind of man would do such a thing to anybody, especially to his wife? Although she had become accustomed to Bruiser's abuse, he had never locked her in a room or restrained her movements before.

Like a cornered rabbit, she became nearly as rageful as he had been. She pounded on the door but no one came to free her. As far away from the main buildings as she was, she doubted anybody could hear her anyway. Despite this, she continued.

Even if someone did hear her, she doubted anyone would be foolish enough to defy Bruiser and open the door to free her. Everybody knew he had a bad temper.

Changing her strategy, she jiggled the handle, trying to pry it open, but it wouldn't budge. Finally, in desperation, she pulled and tugged at it furiously. She did this intermittently for hours but it wouldn't give. Left there for the afternoon with no change of clothes and no food, she became tired. Weary from travel and her travail, her fury finally abated.

She wanted and needed to get out but the lock remained firm. She came to realize her imprisonment was calculated and purposeful. She was being kept in the dark because of the "emergency" at the compound, whatever that happened to be.

As evening approached, no one arrived to give her food. With the refrigerator and cabinets empty, there was absolutely nothing worthwhile to eat in the bungalow and she had become very hungry.

She might as well have been a prisoner at San Quentin. Her solitary confinement lasted that entire day and night. Sleeping intermittently and restlessly, she got up numerous times to check on the door. It remained locked. Her husband never returned to come to bed either. This didn't surprise her, nor did it displease her. As angry with him as she had become, his absence was a relief.

Finally, after having fallen into a fitful sleep for several hours, she arose late the following morning. She was tired, stiff, hungry and pissed. Trying the door once again, it was still locked. In her fury, she jiggled the handle furiously but this time something clicked and it opened instantly. The lock was still engaged but her constant prying had loosened the frame enough for the lock to have become compromised. This set her free.

Since it was 9:45 the following morning, the sun was already beating down, adding to her hunger and crankiness. Although partially dressed with yesterday's clothing and having a slight headache, she knew what she needed—a cup of coffee. Not having eaten anything other than pretzels and peanuts on the plane since her croissant the day before, she headed straight to the kitchen to get a cup of coffee. Hopefully, she would find something left over from breakfast to eat. Even a stale piece of toast or a bowl of cereal would help. She desperately needed to put something into her empty stomach.

Having walked around the pool, she headed up the five steps that led to the kitchen. When she reached the breezeway landing, she was startled by a loud grunt coming from behind her. It sounded like the noise a weightlifter might make while trying to bench press or dead lift heavy weight.

Instinctively, she stopped. Although nearly frozen by the unexpected sound, she turned around. When she did, she spotted two huge men. They were just a few feet away from her and they were carrying a woman.

Being completely focused on what they were doing, neither man spotted her. One man was on each side of the woman they were transporting, supporting her torso rather than carrying her from head and foot. They had come out of Daren Magnus's master bedroom through the sliding glass door. Never having seen these men at the compound before, Emily wondered who they were, but she certainly didn't ask. She was too cautious for that. Instinctively, she knew not to speak nor to allow her presence to become known. Instead, she kept completely still, refusing to permit herself to be seen.

She was so scared by what was happening that she wished she had remained locked in her bungalow, but that was no longer possible. Fortunately, the men were too busy with the woman they were carrying to pay attention to anything else. While they were tightening their grip, Emily used the moment to slide further into the shadow of the pillar in the archway between the living area and the kitchen.

Once safely secluded, she took a much better look at what was happening. To say the men were huge doesn't do justice to just how large they were. Each was enormous, nearly as large as a sumo wrestler.

Taking a much better look at both of them from the safety of her concealed position, Emily was certain she had never seen either of these men before. As large and sinister looking as they were, she was certain she would not have forgotten them. In addition to being gigantic, they were also creepy—the kind of men vulnerable women instinctively know to avoid.

After appraising them, she took a much better look at the young woman they were carrying. This is when she realized that it was not a woman at all. It was an underage girl, a teenager. She was certain of this because she knew the girl. Although Emily couldn't remember the girl's name, the teen had worked at Fisherman's North Drop as a hostess. Emily remembered how gregarious and talkative the girl had been but, for the life of her, she couldn't remember the girl's name.

Perhaps this was because the restaurant went through numerous hostesses. The rest of the restaurant staff was consistent but not the hostesses. Emily remembered this girl though. Tall and pale, she had long black hair, but now, with the two goons carrying her, the girl's hair fell back and nearly touched the ground. The teen's face was leaning back, looking skyward but it also pointed away from Emily. The girl was wearing a short black, V-neck, half-sleeve dress and ballet slippers. Because her legs were so long, the girl's feet dragged on the ground. This caused the slippers to dislodge and fall off.

When this happened, Daren Magnus bolted out of his bedroom in his underwear. He was wearing nothing other than a pair of blue striped boxer shorts. Infuriated, he picked up the two slippers and threw them at the young woman who couldn't have been a day older than sixteen. She might have even been younger than that. When Daren threw the slippers, he did so angrily. Both of them hit the girl solidly. One hit her right in the face but the girl didn't move. She didn't even flinch. In fact, she didn't move or react to anything, probably because she couldn't.

Daren bragged that he "liked to hurt it," meaning a woman's vagina, but his rage at this underage girl was the first evidence Emily had ever seen of his aberrant proclivity. It was terrifying.

Watching from the shadows, Emily began to come to grips with what was actually taking place. Although she knew she was witnessing the aftermath of a crime, she was unable to study the situation fully because, out of the corner of her eye, she saw her enraged husband. Spotting her, he materialized out of nowhere, moving toward her at lightning speed. When he reached Emily a split second later, he pushed her violently.

Jolted by the force of the blow, Emily twisted and stumbled, but she instinctively knew better than to fall to the ground. She refused to lose her balance. Using all of the dexterity she developed through years of ballet, she kept her feet. She had to. She knew that if she fell, Bruiser would kick her while she was down. Since he had done this to her numerous times in the past, she was certain he would do it again. Given the situation, even Daren's presence wouldn't stop him.

Instead of protesting or remaining to ask questions about what she had witnessed, she abandoned her need for food and coffee. Moving quickly, without hesitation, she retreated to her bungalow. Reaching it in record time, she dutifully locked herself in the room by twisting the lock on the outside of the door, resetting it. In stark terror, she sat on the edge of the bed. Although trying to be motionless and serene, she shook like a leaf. Her heart raced so fast that it was difficult for her to breathe.

Understanding what she had just seen, she could neither process it nor believe it. Was the girl alive or dead? She couldn't be sure but in her heart she felt certain the girl wasn't alive. This had to be what the "emergency" was all about.

This meant that what happened to this girl must have been planned. No other explanation made sense. What other reason could there be? What happened to this young girl had to have been premeditated. It could not have been random—not just something that went wrong. That wasn't possible. Try as she might, she couldn't rationalize or excuse what she had just witnessed.

The girl had been murdered, and Daren Magnus was behind it. He must have been. Nothing else made sense. The girl was carried out of Daren's bedroom. No ambulance was called and no attempt at resuscitation was made. Had the girl been alive, they would have tried to save her, but they didn't.

The two giant men must have been "cleaners" like the ones she had seen on episodes of The Sopranos or numerous gangster movies. It was their job to erase any evidence that the girl had ever been at Estate Viol.

But what about her husband? Emily was forced to ask herself about his involvement. What was his part in all of this? When he called her, did he know what was about to happen or didn't he? She also wondered if he had been an active participant. She hoped he hadn't been but was just a facilitator instead.

She didn't know, but the thought of what she had just witnessed suddenly overwhelmed her. It made her sick to her stomach. Despite not having had anything to eat in the past twenty-four hours, she raced to the bathroom and vomited numerous times, even though very little came up. Her body simply couldn't handle the shock of what she had just seen.

Knowing better than to try and open the door again, she simply sat there, doing her best to become a completely submissive wife, but this was difficult. Her mind continued to race. She tried to settle her stomach by breathing slowly but, as traumatized as she had become, it was a losing battle.

Having seen for herself what the "emergency" was, Emily began to piece together other things that had perplexed her for a long time. In Daren's bedroom, for example, a massive safe had been built into the floor. She knew this because Bruiser had mentioned it several times.

The safe was filled with cash, fraudulent IDs, military grade weapons and numerous high-end watches. Although she had always been kept at arms-length from the safe and its contents, she knew exactly what it contained. Now she understood the reason why Daren kept all of these weapons and valuables at his immediate disposal. Suddenly, everything made sense.

Like Jeffrey Epstein, who Daren knew and referred to as "the gray-haired dude," Magnus had kept substantial valuables in close proximity just in case his perverse behavior was discovered. This way, if his deviant proclivities ever became known, he could simply disappear and escape justice. With weapons, funds and fake identification, he could simply vanish and begin a new life without ever missing a beat. So far, this had been unnecessary, but now there was a witness, her!

Only Daren, Bruiser and a few others had access to the safe and its contents. Piecing all of this together, Emily felt certain that Daren, Bruiser and their associates were deeply involved in sex trafficking and had been for quite some time. Sitting there on her bed, she wondered how many other girls might had left Estate Viol by being stuffed into the back of a SUV by those two huge cleaners.

At the same time, she really didn't want to know. What she wanted was for it to have never happened. Sitting there on the edge of her bed, her only option was to wait for her husband to come and let her out, which he did several hours later.

When he finally arrived and opened the door, Bruiser walked in with her luggage and carryon bag in hand. He placed them on the bed. Turning to her with a smile, he said, "Your lunch is waiting in the dining room. Eat it quickly, take a shower and be ready to leave by 3:30 sharp. You're needed at the restaurant a little early today."

Once he provided her with direction, which was accompanied with a pleasant smile, he turned and left their bungalow. He acted just as if nothing had happened. To most, this might seem bizarre, but she knew this would be the way Bruiser chose to handle the situation. Avoiding reality was definitely Bruiseresque behavior.

Complying, doing precisely what she had been directed to do, Emily ate, showered and was ready to be driven to work at 3:30 p.m., on the dot, just like it was a normal day. For her, tacit compliance to Bruiser's demand was also Emilyesque.

From that moment forward, Bruiser never mentioned a word about what happened. He never referred to it in any way, not one time ever. By behaving this way, he gave Emily another command, a silent one. Despite being unspoken, she understood the intent of his demand perfectly. She knew she was never to broach the subject of what happened to that girl, not ever. This was a demand she understood and obeyed without deviation.

Emily remained silent about what happened for the next fifteen years. She continued to remain silent, even after the couple eventually divorced. This is how intimidated she had become. She refused to breach their no-talk rule even though it put her at odds with her deeply-held, conservative Jewish values. She probably would have remained silent forever if it hadn't been for the arrest of Jeffrey Epstein in the spring of 2019. The extensive media coverage of this event, along with the stories about what had happened to so many of Epstein's victims, provided her with the courage she needed to come forward. Her conscience would no longer allow her to remain silent.

CHAPTER 2

An Enigma Wrapped in a Conundrum

JULY 2019

One evening, after having just finished penning my most recent book, I was sitting at my desk wondering what my next writing project would be. With a lifetime goal of authoring thirty books, I was well on his way to accomplishing my goal, but I didn't like the feeling of not having a solid idea about what to write next. While writing a political post on Facebook, my cellphone began its melodious chant. Looking at the screen to see who was calling, I saw Emily Goldfarb's name flash on the screen. She was a divorcée who had retaken her maiden name. I had known her for many years.

Having met on Match.com, we actually dated a few times. Emily was a beautiful woman. Short and trim, she had deep blue eyes, short black hair and an enchanting, exotic allure about her that made her a successful model many years earlier. Best of all, she was smart, well-read and seemed to have solid values. Although there was a certain level of chemistry between us, she and I never became truly romantic. Instead, we became fast friends.

Not having spoken with her in several years, although we did keep in touch with each other regularly through social media on Facebook, I was surprised to see her name on my iPhone screen.

Smiling as I answered, I said, "Hi Emily, nice to hear from you. How have you been?" Expecting her to respond pleasantly, I was surprised to hear distress and sadness in her voice.

"I suppose I am doing all right, but my heart is very troubled," Emily responded.

Recognizing this was a serious call and not just a friendly conversation where we would catch up, I replied. "What's the matter?"

"It's this whole Jeffrey Epstein thing. Watching it on the news has really gotten me upset," Emily acknowledged.

"I understand completely," I replied, as my mind flashed to the arrest of financier Jeffrey Epstein that had become headline news several days earlier. Epstein had been apprehended when he returned home from being in Paris.

"Yes, but what has me upset goes much deeper than what's being reported on the news."

Instinctively knowing Emily had something significant to discuss, I waited for her to continue.

"Jack, you're the only person I know that I can trust."

Surprised to hear this, I didn't respond other than to say, "Thank you." I suspected she had a great deal more to divulge.

"I've been keeping a secret for fifteen years and it's killing me. The only one who knows what I am about to tell you is my mother, and she's bedridden, nearly blind and in need of constant care."

Once Emily made this statement, she couldn't help herself. She began to cry. Knowing not to interrupt, I waited patiently for her to regain her composure, which she did shortly thereafter.

Taking a deep breath, Emily continued by explaining the reason for her distress. "What Epstein did to those girls was pure evil. Watching the story unfold has triggered some things I have deep inside me. You see, I have my own story to tell about what happened on Saint Thomas."

"You do?"

"That's right, and it's just as bad and perverted as what Epstein has done. In some ways, maybe it's even worse, if that's possible."

I was truly surprised but knew better than to interrupt. Instinctively, I realized she was just getting started.

Emily said, "Epstein is actually a part of my story, but I'll get to that later."

Once Epstein's name was mentioned as an actual participant and not simply as a passing reference, my attention soared. Being a writer, I knew to pay careful attention to every word Emily was divulging.

After listening to Emily's entire mesmerizing tale about what happened the day of the "emergency" at Estate Viol, which was accompanied by several tearful outbursts, it was my turn to take a deep breath. My mind was racing. I had so many questions that it was difficult to know where to begin.

My first was the most obvious one. "When they carried the girl to the Toyota SUV and loaded her into the back of it, do you think was dead or still alive?"

"I'm not sure Jack, but she was very pale," Emily responded.

"Pale or gray?" I asked.

"Ashen," Emily replied.

Measuring my words, I added. "That's probably because a corpse loses its color quickly. I'm pretty sure the girl was dead."

"I hadn't thought about that part of it, about her lack of color. Since there was no blood coming from any visible wound, I hoped she was alive, but you're probably right. What makes me suspect she was dead was she didn't have any response when her slippers were thrown at her. She didn't recoil or wince, and Daren threw them very hard," Emily added.

"But you never saw that girl again, right?" I asked, almost rhetorically.

"No, never. That's another reason why I believe she was dead. It's also the reason why those huge men were there. They were 'cleaners' who were supposed to take care of things. I believe they were called to erase any evidence she had ever been present at the Magnus compound."

"This is unbelievable. It's just like a movie," I replied in dismay. After a long silence, I asked. "What do you think they did with her body?"

"I've wondered about that hundreds of times. I don't know, not for sure, but I do have a theory."

"What is it?"

"The restaurant that Bruiser and I ran for Daren was called Fisherman's North Drop. The name is important. The restaurant actually sits on the top of a hill with a balcony jutting out, 120 feet high on a cliff overlooking the Caribbean Sea. It's truly a picturesque setting on Saint Thomas."

"So, you think they threw the girl over the balcony?" I asked, half joking.

"That's precisely what I think." Emily added, "but that's not all. The restaurant was named Fisherman's North Drop for a reason. It's where fishermen dropped their nets to catch fish. It was their 'north drop.'"

"Hmmm, interesting," I replied half-heatedly, not following why this tidbit of information was significant.

Filling in the gap, Emily added. "Because that's where the fish are, it's also the feeding ground for sharks."

"Oh my God!" I exclaimed, horrified by the implications of what I had just learned.

"But that's not all, Jack. This fate may have happened to a lot more girls. While I was managing Fisherman's North Drop, we had at least fifty different hostesses. None of them ever lasted very long. The rest of the staff, including the waitresses, busboys and chef, remained consistent but there was a constant turnover in hostesses."

Taking a deep breath, she proceeded. "All of the hostesses were underage. That's the way Daren liked them, underage."

"Holy crap," I exclaimed. As infuriated as I was, I couldn't help being crude. After another long moment of silence, as I thought about the ramifications of what she had just said, I asked. "But wouldn't there be reports about these girls being missing? How could something like this have happened to so many girls? It just seems implausible to me."

"This is where Daren's well-orchestrated scheme became complicated. This didn't just happen. It was systematically planned." She conjectured, "What he created was a carefully contrived scheme to lure underage girls off of the mainland and bring them to Saint Thomas for sex."

Emily continued. "Once they arrived, being flown to Saint Thomas on one of Daren's two private planes, they were forced to have sex with him and his friends. Magnus's operation was just like what Epstein was doing—the exact same thing."

Based on how reverently Daren spoke about Epstein, Emily added, "Daren was an Epstein clone. He kept the girls in bungalows like mine, where the locks were on the outside of the door and not on the inside. This made their bungalows jail cells, just like mine was." Emily suspected this was also "the place where Daren's friends had sex with them." According to her, once they were inside, there was no way for them to escape.

"This is an unbelievable story," I replied after a long moment to allow what I had heard to sink in. Taking a deep breath, I asked. "So, what you are telling me is everything Daren Magnus did was meticulously planned and coordinated? It wasn't random or spur-of-the-moment?"

"That's exactly what I am telling you," Emily exclaimed. "It was more than planned. It was choreographed to perfection."

"But what I can't come to grips with is how all of this could have happened. How could they have gotten away with this for so long?"

Answering, Emily said, "Daren is very arrogant. He didn't think he would ever get caught. He believed he was too smart for that."

"His scheme was brilliant. I'll give him that," I interjected. "Diabolical but brilliant."

"You're right," Emily agreed. "Nearly all of the girls came from the panhandle area of north Florida. They were runaways, so they wouldn't be missed. Daren had a woman who recruited these girls—just like Epstein had. Daren's 'Ghislaine' had been in the Navy. She lived in Rosemary Beach, so recruited girls from that area of Florida, from Pensacola to Destin to Panama City."

"So, you're saying Daren Magnus had an accomplice? Are you sure about this?"

"Absolutely," Emily affirmed.

"Do you know her name?"

"No, I don't. I've tried to remember a thousand times, but I just can't."

"Okay," I responded, "but keep trying."

"Let me describe to you exactly how their recruitment system worked." Becoming very focused, Emily explained. "Once a runaway girl was spotted in Pensacola, Destin or Panama City, Daren's woman would ask if the girl wanted a seasonal job as a hostess at a swanky restaurant in the Virgin Islands. As an incentive to get the girl to come, Daren's accomplice would offer the girl free room and board. This was quite an enticement because it would seem much safer to these girls than continuing to live on the street."

"So, these girls would actually look at what was being offered as an answer to prayer," I reasoned, trying to put myself in their position. To them, "it seemed like a safe situation. Plus, because Daren's accomplice was a young, pretty woman making the offer, they felt safe by responding favorably. Is that how it worked?"

"Bingo," Emily confirmed. "But she did more than that. To lure these girls, she showed them a large diamond ring she was wearing, telling them Daren had purchased it for her."

"He bought her a diamond engagement ring?" I asked. "But, wasn't he already married? Why would he do that?"

"I've wondered about that myself. I don't know for sure," Emily admitted.

Trying to help, I speculated. "Maybe it was just a showpiece, something to make the marked girl believe Daren was a 'Prince Charming' type of guy."

"You might be right," Emily mused. "I've never thought of that."

"It might have added to her credibility. Plus, it would also say, 'He's already taken.' That would put each of the girls at ease about the potential of being sexually exploited, wouldn't it?"

"Yes, it would," Emily admitted. "As an enticement to come, each was told that, as a hostess, she would meet some very wealthy people at Fisherman's North Drop. These potential benefactors would sponsor the girl to become an actress, a model or whatever the girl wanted to be. Thinking this would be the adventure of a lifetime, it wasn't difficult to get them to say, 'Yes,' especially being as young and naïve as they were."

To clarify, I asked. "Once the girl arrived at the Magnus compound, she was placed in a bungalow exactly like yours. Isn't that correct?"

"Yes, some of them anyway. Others stayed in cheap housing paid for by Daren."

I continued to piece things together. "So, for the girls placed in the bungalows, once one was locked inside, the trap was sprung and her fate was sealed. She had no recourse other than to be sexually compliant."

"Precisely," Emily replied. "They were prisoners in those bungalows, just like I was."

"Emily, what kind of person would even come up with an idea like this? It's so depraved," I added.

"The bungalows were actually self-contained prison cells." Some of the girls were "kept there at night to have sex with Daren and his friends," while others were housed at Villa Papillon. A few were actually housed at the Ritz.

"So, believing they were about to be saved by a generous benefactor, these lost, troubled underage girls fell for this scheme hook, line and sinker. They became sex slaves. This is what you are telling me, isn't it?"

"That's precisely what I am telling you," Emily affirmed.

Thinking it through like I was the detective, Sean Kincannon, from my Moon Series novels, I asked. "But how could Daren get them into

Saint Thomas? Wouldn't they need a passport or some other kind of identification to get onto the island?" Without waiting for her to answer, I asked another question. "There would have to have been some sort of record of these girls traveling to Saint Thomas but never returning, right?"

Filling in the pieces, Emily explained. "Jack, this was the genius of Daren's scheme. Saint Thomas is American territory. This means no passport, driver's license or any other kind of identification would be required for a plane coming from the United States. It would be like flying from Nashville to Chicago."

"Right, I didn't think about that. Daren thought of everything, didn't he?" I conceded grudgingly.

"He certainly did," Emily admitted. "Daren's entire operation was very sophisticated and extremely well-coordinated. He had two planes—two big planes. Both were capable of non-stop flights from Nashville to Saint Thomas. They liked to refer to their operation as 'Air Daren.'"

"Clever," I acknowledged wryly.

"Yes, they thought so too. I was never allowed to fly on Air Daren, not even once. I was always required to fly on Delta or American Airlines. Daren kept his two planes at Banks Aviation, which is located at John C Tune Airport."

"But what about airport security?" I asked.

Emily explained. "Like all airports," JWN has "security cameras everywhere, including inside the stand-alone hanger Daren Magnus rented for his two planes."

"I'm not following," Jack admitted.

"Hang on, you will," Emily explained. "Magnus had all of the security cameras inside his hanger disabled so that nobody could tell who came and who went from the hanger. This also meant nobody would ever know who boarded either of Daren's planes."

During another conversation, Emily went into greater detail about both of Magnus's airplanes. The largest one was a G5, the kind rappers frequently mention in their songs. Magnus's luxurious G5, which was actually owned by one of his companies, for tax reasons, could seat as many as forty. It was the largest private plane that flew into Saint Thomas other than Epstein's 737, the *Lolita Express*.

Because Magnus's G5 was so large, it wouldn't fit into the hanger. It was too tall. Privacy about who boarded the G5 being paramount, Daren had a hydraulic system installed so that the shocks could be manually deflated. Doing this lowered the height of the plane enough for it to fit comfortably in the hangar.

I had no idea that such a thing was even possible but, when I heard about this, it indicated a level of intentionality about his sex trafficking and pedophilia that was deeply disturbing. It made me wonder if sexual asphyxiation was Magnus's true aphrodisiac. If so, then having the G5 located in the hangar would be necessary for him to get away with murder. If this was Magnus's purpose for the hydraulic system, then it was a wise investment. It allowed him to pursue every aspect of his perversion successfully for many years.

Magnus's second plane was a Hawker. Much smaller, it could seat about fifteen people, but it was even more luxurious than the G5. The Hawker was very fast and equally as expensive. Other than when Daren flew in numerous people for his parties, the Hawker was the aircraft he used most frequently. When it was used, like the G5, the boarding process was done inside the hangar.

Returning to the conversation, I said. "Let me see if I understand exactly how Daren's operation worked. When these girls agreed to travel to Saint Thomas, they would be driven inside the hangar by car. Once inside, they were out of sight of any of JWN's surveillance cameras, correct?"

"Correct," Emily acknowledged.

"Then, because Daren had disabled his own cameras, there would be no record of the girls getting out of the car and onto the plane. They would just board the G5 or Hawker without be spotted by anybody. Is that correct?"

"Yes."

I continued to put the pieces together. "So, nobody would know or even suspect that anything was wrong or illegal. Isn't that right?"

"Precisely. Having private airplanes was the key to Daren's entire operation. Since nobody knew who was on the plane when it took off, once it was in the air, the fate of these girls was sealed. Each was completely in Daren's power. They never suspected a thing until it was too late."

Shaking my head in dismay, I concluded, "They didn't even need to be coaxed, did they?"

"Nope," Emily agreed.

"Being enticed by a private, luxurious airplane headed for the tropics, they would jump at the chance to go, wouldn't they?"

"Yes, and many did."

I continued. "Thinking everything was on the up-and-up, believing they were being saved from their grim situations, they thought their prayers were being answered, didn't they?"

"Yes, that's how deceived they were."

"None of them had a clue about what was in store for them, did they?"

"Not a one. That's how I see it, anyway," Emily concurred. "Magnus had a continuous supply of runaway, underage girls. Believing the lies they were told by his 'pretend fiancée,' these unsuspecting girls came to Daren's compound on Saint Thomas willingly, eagerly. Nobody knew they were there either—not the law, not the girls' parents, not anybody."

She waited for a long moment for me to respond to what she said, but I was too overwhelmed to say anything. Instead, I just sat quietly on the other end of the phone trying to process everything I had heard.

After a long moment, I finally asked, "How many girls do you think there were in all?" Reflecting, I added, "And do you think he is still doing this?"

"I don't know, Jack. I really don't, but I have remained quiet about this for far too long. Daren sold his place in the Virgin Islands though. That I know," she declared. "I've been afraid they would kill me if I ever opened my mouth." Clarifying herself, she continued. "No, I'm not afraid they would kill me; I'm terrified they would!"

"I can see why," I replied, concurring with Emily's rationale for being fearful.

"If they knew I was talking to you, I'm sure they would have me killed. There's no doubt in my mind whatsoever."

"I believe you," I replied. "I think they would too, but why do you think they allowed you to stay alive back then . . . back when you witnessed that girl being hauled off?"

"I've wondered about that a million times," Emily admitted.

"When you watched that girl being taken away, you became a real threat. If they were going to kill you, that would have been the time to do it, not now."

"Perhaps they were worried about having to explain my disappearance," Emily reasoned. "I certainly wasn't a runaway. I had a ticket on Delta Airlines and had passed through a major airport. There were surveillance cameras all over the place at Nashville International, especially back then, it being so close to 9/11."

"That makes sense," I admitted.

"Jack, I wasn't an untraceable runaway, and I worked where the bodies were dumped. Killing me would have been very risky. The last thing they wanted was for the cops to be snooping around Estate Viol or Fisherman's North Drop."

"That definitely makes sense," I concurred.

"But there might have been another reason," Emily added.

"What?"

"When Bruiser and I finally did get divorced, Daren was one of the first men to call and ask me out." Waiting a long moment, she added. "He wanted to take me out on a date."

Hearing this unexpected response, I couldn't help myself. I burst out laughing. Emily did too.

We needed the laughter. A moment later, I said. "You can't be serious?"

Emily didn't reply. Although I couldn't see her face, I suspected she was smiling coquettishly, the way pretty women do when they answer a question without saying a word.

"What a twist," I replied. "So, you're telling me you think you survived because Daren wanted to date you. For him, that would have meant having sex with you, right?"

"Probably," she responded, "But he never did. I promise you that."

"I believe you. The guy's a monster. It took a lot of gall for him to even ask; don't you think?"

"Yes, I would never go out with him. Just the thought of it," Emily began, but she never finished her sentence. Instead, her voice quivered.

As the telephone conversation was winding down, I sat there quietly processing what I had learned. Finally, I concluded. "What a story. These guys are deviants. We need to go to the FBI with this."

"Maybe," Emily replied. "I know I need to come forward, but I'm scared to death. Just watching the stuff about Epstein on TV has made me realize what I need to do, but I don't trust the FBI. I just don't—not after all of the corruption that's been in the news about what they've done the last couple of years. This is why I called you. You're the only person I know that I can trust with this."

Mirroring her apprehension about the FBI, I responded carefully. "With the corruption we've learned about Comey, McCabe, Strzok and the others, I don't trust the Bureau either, especially when I read about that 'sweetheart deal' Epstein got back when all of this was happening. The original court case about Epstein happened about the same time as this, didn't it?"

"Yes," Emily affirmed. "This whole thing is awful. That's why I called. I didn't know what else to do. I still don't, do you?"

"No," I replied. "Not for sure, but I do think there's a way to bring all of this out in the open and remain safe. I think we can force the FBI to play it straight with us."

"How?"

"I might have an idea," I suggested tentatively.

"Let's hear it," Emily asked eagerly.

Taking a deep breath, I said, "What if I write about this and make a book out of it? I would write it in real time. That way, we can create our own audience. Quite a few people would read it. That would be good for us. There is safety in numbers."

Emily was intrigued. She encouraged me to continue explaining my idea.

"If enough people pay attention, and I think they will, we can expose what occurred on Saint Thomas, bring justice to what happened to that girl who was carried away by the two cleaners and also ensure our survival. What do you think?"

Although frightened by the prospect of going public, knowing how dangerous it would be, Emily replied. "I love it. I think it's a great idea."

"Good, then I'll get started writing immediately. This is too important to delay."

"By the way," Emily added, "What I've told you is just the tip of the iceberg. Part of the story actually involves Epstein himself and an attempt to defraud the U.S. Treasury out of millions of dollars in taxes."

"Of course, it does, Emily," I replied sarcastically. "I would have expected nothing less. What we have on Saint Thomas is an enigma wrapped in a conundrum. One thing I know for sure is once we get started we will be embarking on the roller coaster ride of a lifetime."

THE THREE COMMAS CLUB

CHAPTER 3

He Did Cross the Line

JULY 2019

Three days after our extensive telephone conversation, I met Emily at a local Starbucks in Cool Springs. My purpose was to learn more about what happened on Saint Thomas, to fill in details and to discuss what steps needed to be taken to bring justice to those troubling events fifteen years earlier.

When I walked in, Emily was already seated at a corner table. After we greeted each other, I went to the counter to order a Grande Very Berry Hibiscus, with lemonade instead of water. Other than sweet tea, a Southern staple, this was my favorite summertime beverage. All Emily wanted was a tall black coffee.

Returning with our drinks in hand a short time later, I noticed Emily had remained as attractive as she had been the first time I met her more than ten years earlier. Some women retain their looks well into middle age and Emily was certainly one of them. Still trim, she was wearing a tasteful black dress that hung off of her left shoulder. Accented by several turquoise rings, with matchings bracelets and a necklace, this well-coordinated outfit set off her brilliant blue eyes magnificently.

As pretty as Emily looked though, based on her countenance it was obvious she was deeply troubled. Given the topic of our impending discussion, this didn't surprise me in the least. Because it was her nature to always dress fashionably, even though this was just a meeting at Starbucks, the attractiveness of her appearance couldn't conceal how troubled she was.

Emily's complete attention was focused on the ramifications of what would eventuate from disclosing her deeply-held secret to another human being. On the outside, she looked poised and confident but, on the inside where it really counts, she was clearly disturbed.

Spotting this instantly, I modified my demeanor accordingly. Looking at her, knowing she had struggled with insomnia for many years, I asked, "Have you been able to sleep?"

Laughing that I had remembered, she replied. "Not at all. Since we talked a couple of days ago, I've barely slept a wink."

"I was afraid of that but I'm not surprised. I think it will get better once you get through debriefing me about the rest of what happened." I said this, although I wasn't sure it was true. I did my best to reassure her though.

"That is, if I survive," she replied somewhat dramatically.

"You're going to survive," I replied confidently, but Emily remained unconvinced.

She countered. "This is what I want. I need to be put in the Witness Protection Program. That's the only way I can know for certain that I will make it through this." Looking at me appraisingly, she asked, "Do you think I would qualify?"

"Probably," I answered, although I had no idea what the criteria was to be accepted into the federal Witness Protection Program. Trying to redirect the conversation away from what might happen to what actually had happened on Saint Thomas, I said. "What I do know is we must put everything that's in your head down on paper. Without doing this, we have nothing."

Emily agreed. "I know you're right but this is very difficult for me."

"Once I have the complete story and understand it thoroughly, we will have enough to take your story to a journalist. If we do that, rather than go directly to the FBI, the Bureau will not be able to bury it like the events that surrounded Jeffrey Epstein's fiasco back in 2007." Having read about what happened to Epstein years earlier, I added. "It was Florida's law enforcement that actually buried it though and not the FBI."

After taking a sip of my drink, I looked at her. "Did you ever think you would live to see the day that the FBI couldn't be trusted to protect a woman like you?"

"Never," she responded contemptuously.

"Me neither, but this is where we are." With a look of determination, I added. "Okay, it's time to get started."

Looking at me appraisingly, Emily said. "I hope you don't think I'm being overly dramatic. My fear is real. If they knew I had said anything to you, breaking my de facto vow of silence, my life would definitely be in danger. I'm not exaggerating."

I believed her, but I must have conveyed a nuance of skepticism concerning how serious the threat to her actually was. At least, this was how Emily interpreted my non-verbal response. She just looked at me for a long moment, making me feel somewhat uncomfortable. Pondering how to proceed, she made the decision to disclose even more about what she had experienced.

She said, "Bruiser has struck me many times, Jack. Most of the time he was content to be verbally abusive, but he did cross the line on numerous occasions. I'm not exaggerating."

"I know you're not," I replied, but my demeanor continued to be perceived as less than being convinced. At least, this is how Emily interpreted what I was thinking.

To prove her point, she said. "Let me tell you a story. There was one incident that stands out above all others. It illustrates just how physically abusive Bruiser could be. It occurred one evening when the two of us left Fisherman's North Drop after closing the restaurant. This was back in December, 2005."

Although I wasn't certain what Emily was going to divulge, I knew it was critically important to follow closely. So, I sat back, took a sip of my Very Berry Hibiscus and listened.

"It began just before closing. It was very, very late at night. We were on the north side of the island where the restaurant was located. It's considered to be the 'residential area,' but there were only bad neighborhoods between the restaurant and the Magnus compound. When I say bad, I mean really bad and quite dangerous."

"I get it," I interjected. "You had to go through the rough part of town to get to the restaurant."

"Precisely." Looking off for a long moment, she changed directions. "Jack, when Bruiser got angry, his eyes turned black. I could no longer see the brown in them and I always knew what that meant."

Taking a sip of coffee, with trembling hands, she continued. "Returning home that night, I was terrified as our SUV screeched around sharp curves. We were going too fast for the mountainside road. Bruiser had been drinking Johnny Walker Black all night. He began about 7 p.m., so he had already had quite a bit to drink. It was about 2 a.m. before we left. This means he had a drink in his hand for at least seven hours. He was definitely intoxicated. We got into a terrible fight about the way Daren was defrauding the government with his taxes. I was afraid this would make us vulnerable too."

"You haven't told me anything about that," I interrupted.

"I know I haven't," Emily apologized. "We'll get to that soon enough but I want to explain—to help you understand—exactly why I am still afraid of my ex-husband's vengeance."

"Okay, I'm sorry to have cut you off. You were saying?"

"I'm trying to give you the best example of Bruiser's brutality that I can," Emily explained. "In his anger toward me for challenging anything about Daren Magnus's activities, he reached across the seat where I was sitting and opened the passenger door. Once he had it open, he threw me out of the SUV, while it was still moving."

"What!" I exclaimed. This clearly startled me.

"You heard me. He threw me out of the car, literally threw me out."

"How fast were you going?" I asked, obviously disturbed by what I had just learned. A moment later, before she could respond, I asked a follow-up question. "What about your seatbelt? Weren't you wearing it?"

"No, I wasn't," Emily admitted. "As I hit the rocky pavement, the door to the Toyota Forerunner swung back and hit my thigh very hard, nearly breaking the largest bone in my body. My left femur sustained a severe bone bruise. Oblivious to my pain and injury, Bruiser kept on driving. He never stopped and he never returned. He just left me there on the side of the road."

"Like you were garbage!" I exclaimed, angered by what Emily had just divulged. Before learning this, I had considered Emily's husband to be a brute, but I never suspected he was as violent and vicious as he actually was.

"But that's not all," Emily continued. "It gets worse, much worse. He left me sitting on the side of the road in a crime filled neighborhood in the middle of the night. I was so scared. I was hurt and all alone. The road didn't even have streetlights. It was pitch black."

"How long did you sit there?"

"I'm not sure. Quite a while," Emily admitted. "I kept thinking he would circle back to get me, but he never did."

"How unconscionable," I interjected.

Fighting back tears, Emily paused for a long minute before continuing. "Finally, I managed to get up. With no other option, I walked back to Estate Viol. It took me quite a while. I was in a great deal of pain. I arrived about 5 a.m. When I called out for my husband, he refused to open the gate. He wouldn't let me in. Because my leg was injured, I couldn't climb over the wrought iron gate or the cement wall either."

"What did you do?" I asked.

"I just sat there crying," Emily explained. "Finally, the estate's maid, who was already up, let me in. When she did, she ran away—literally ran away. My husband was still awake drinking Johnny Walker Black. He hadn't passed out yet. When he saw that I was on 'Daren's estate,' that's when the real terror began."

"The real terror?" I interrupted, unable to restrain my revulsion about what Emily's husband had already done to her. "There's more?"

"Lots more. Because I was unable to run away from Bruiser, he followed me when I walked into our bungalow. That's when the torture began." When she said this, she couldn't help herself. She began to weep.

Knowing not to interrupt, I reproached myself for having had the slightest doubt about how serious Emily's abuse must had been. Penitent and reproachful, I sat there patiently waiting for her to regain her composure.

Several minutes later, she sighed, took a deep breath, a sip of coffee and, after having dried her eyes, continued. While crying, she made a decision about what she would divulge and what she would refrain from disclosing.

Finally, she continued. "I cannot speak about some of the things that happened late that night and into the morning. They are just too painful, but I actually died, at least a piece of me died. I came to the place where I no longer cared. I just couldn't fight anymore. As my husband continued to beat me, I felt myself go somewhere else. I gave up. I felt my soul begin to leave my body, as strange as that might sound. It was that awful. I was bleeding so badly from some of the things he did that he finally became scared that I might die."

"This is an unbelievable story," I interjected. I believed what she was telling me, every word of it. Emily's apprehension was based on legitimate fear. She had a genuine right to be scared. Sitting there, I finally grasped precisely how frightened Emily was about Bruiser's potential retaliation. She was being very courageous to reveal his criminal behavior, knowing it might still put her life at risk.

She returned to her narrative. "Bruiser finally took me to the hospital on the island, where my wounds were sewn up, but I wasn't given any pain killers. I didn't have any anesthetics—none whatsoever—and the person who treated my wounds wasn't even a real physician."

Again, I interrupted, asking how something like this could have happened. It seemed so implausible. "What kind of hospital would allow such a thing?" I asked.

"I didn't go in through the emergency room," She explained. "I went into the hospital through a side door. A lot of money changed hands. Bruiser made a deal with someone. I don't know who it was that sewed me up. I just know it involved a great deal of pain. When the man finished, I was carried to a black SUV. I remember that it had heavily tinted windows. I was very woozy. My memory was sketchy from that point forward because of all the pain from my beating and from the surgery that followed. My body just couldn't take anymore, so it shut down."

"I can't imagine going through something like that," I admitted.

"By the time we ended up back at the estate, it was morning, and my husband had somehow composed himself. He had to. Daren was up, so Bruiser had to behave well, like nothing significant had happened. He wouldn't allow Daren to witness how out of control he had become. That was too dangerous. Instead, he told Daren I was sick. Bruiser said I had probably caught something on the flight down or had eaten something bad and gotten food poisoning. To protect Daren and the others, I was locked up in our bungalow again. This time I didn't mind, even though I didn't have any food or drinkable water. At least I had a bed to lie on. All I had to drink was a Coke, and you cannot imagine how good it tasted. I was so grateful to just have something to drink and to be able to rest."

Smiling, Emily completed her story. "Later that day, I was flown back to Nashville on a commercial airplane to see a real doctor." Looking at me, Emily concluded, "I nearly died. Bruiser nearly killed me. Now, can you see why I have been intimidated into silence for all of these years?"

"Yes," I acknowledged penitently, and I definitely could.

• • •

Emily wanted me to be aware of how vulnerable she was back then and continued to be. What she divulged was an extraordinary account of precisely how far Bruiser would go to intimidate her into remaining silent. Fearful intimidation was his primary weapon and he used it masterfully.

While we were still at Starbucks, Emily wanted to explain why she was required to travel back and forth from Nashville to Saint Thomas so frequently. She wanted me to understand why she and Bruiser were in the restaurant business and what their real purpose was for being in the Virgin Islands in the first place.

Looking at me, she said. "What you have to understand is sex trafficking was what they did for recreation. It was their diversion. It was sport for them, but it definitely was not why Daren bought the $15 million-dollar compound in the Virgin Islands. Raping underage girls was just a pleasant distraction. Magnus's real purpose was to use his new residence to further his business interests and to avoid paying taxes to the federal government."

Emily added. "He wasn't the only one doing this either. There were many others, including Jeffrey Epstein. It's funny but they never referred to Epstein by name. Instead, they spoke of him as 'the gray-haired dude.' It was a term of reverence and endearment."

Appalled, I interrupted. "So, they actually looked up to him for what he was able to get away with?"

"Definitely," Emily affirmed. "They idolized Epstein and some others too. All of these rich men flew their private jets into the airport at Charlotte Amalie. That's what they all had in common. They did this because it was the only airport in the islands with a runway long enough to accommodate their aircraft."

"So, the smaller airports didn't have long enough runways to land the planes, right?" I inquired for clarification.

"That's right. It was like they had a secret fraternity of sex traffickers and tax cheats. All of them were getting away with it. As far as I could tell, there has been no accountability about anything any of them have ever done—at least none that I ever saw." Emily added, "You have to remember, this all happened in the Caribbean, and the islands are very corrupt, including the U.S. Virgin Islands."

Mesmerized by what was being divulged, I sat and listened while Emily explained the entirety of Daren Magnus's devious undertaking. The entire venture began with Daren's desire to get out of his family's business. Originally called West Texas Steak, the business was founded by his grandfather in Waco, TX in 1966. The older Magnus sold it to an oil company in 1972, but bought it back ten years later, renaming the product Always Perfect Prime. Having a natural juiciness that was tasty as well as being more tender than many of its competitors, Always Perfect Prime became a favorite for grillers in the Southwest and eventually nationwide. Best of all, it generated millions for the Magnus family.

Daren's father was rumored to have had mob connections. Whether this was true or not wasn't as important as the fact that Daren was afraid of his father, so fearful that he sued him for his inheritance. It was a brutal lawsuit that Daren eventually won. He received about $50 million as his portion. With this fortune as his starting point, Daren set out to make his mark in the world.

Being the youngest of four brothers, Daren wanted to expand his portfolio beyond Always Perfect Prime, so he set up shop in the Virgin Islands under the umbrella company Viol Enterprises. Utilizing the skills of his Nashville based lawyer, Patrick Bellinger, who was instrumental in putting things together, Daren moved his business dealings to Saint Thomas.

Under Viol Enterprises, there was Connais Ventures, Bay de Grigri, and Fisherman's North Drop restaurant. This is where both Emily and her husband worked. They were also part owners in Leipers Fork Harley in Leipers Fork, Tennessee. This was a company owned by Viol Enterprises. There was an additional Harley dealership that the Chambers weren't involved with that was also owned by Daren Magnus.

Looking at me with a smile, Emily said. "Viol Enterprises was the real reason why we were on the island. For Daren to make his fraudulent scheme work, we were required to spend at least 186 days a year on Saint Thomas, but we had to do more than just be tourists or vacationers. We had to work there. This is the real reason why Daren opened Fisherman's North Drop restaurant. It gave us a valid reason to be there, but it wasn't the true reason to be on Saint Thomas. The real reason was that it allowed Daren to defraud the U.S. Treasury out of millions in tax revenue."

Patrick Bellinger's name appeared on most of the documents. As Daren's lawyer, Bellinger was a frequent guest in Saint Thomas. He came for business and for the parties. Emily knew this because she heard his voice in the background, when Bruiser made a drunk call during one of Daren's parties at the estate.

"How did he do that?" I asked, clearly perplexed.

"By participating in a brilliant tax fraud. That's how," Emily added with a mischievous smile.

CHAPTER 4

The Dam Had Broken

JULY 2019

That evening, as I was sitting in front of my television mindlessly watching a vapid sitcom, my thoughts continued to wander back to the conversation I had with Emily earlier in the afternoon. To say that I was disquieted would be a monumental understatement. Having maintained continuous sobriety in Alcoholics Anonymous for more than a quarter of a century, I believed I had heard just about everything, but I had badly underestimated the gravity of Emily's experience. The level of depravity and violence Emily had both witnessed and experienced went far beyond anything I had ever seen or heard. I was actually floored by what she had divulged.

Having attended thousands of AA and ALANON meetings over the years, I was no stranger to the dark side of human behavior. Despite this, the systematic trafficking of underage girls for sex, coupled with the probable murder of some, disposing of them like they were chum to be fed to sharks, was something I had never expected, especially to have been the experience of someone I knew well.

What she had divulged seemed more like a movie plot than something that could actually happen, but it wasn't. This was real.

While sitting there, my iPhone began its harmonious melody, telling me I had a call. Looking at the screen, hoping it wasn't another invasive telemarketer, I saw that it was Emily.

After saying hello, she told me she had been unable to get the events we discussed out of her mind. Understanding this completely, I knew exactly how she felt. Once she left our meeting at Starbucks, at some point later that afternoon, she decided to reveal even more. Acting upon her decision, she made the call.

"Jack, once I began to open up about what happened, it was like the dam finally broke and a torrent of memories were released. After leaving Starbucks, my mind became flooded with details I've suppressed for so long that I suspected I had actually forgotten some of them. Out of fear and dread, I have put them out of my mind, but I am no longer willing to hide in the shadows. I'm tired of living a half-life, of being intimidated by the evil sexual perversions of men like Daren Magnus and my ex-husband."

Measuring her words, she continued. "I want to be free. I want to have a real life. I'm calling because I want to finish the story I started this afternoon. I want to tell you the rest of what happened that night. Do you have a few minutes?"

Knowing how therapeutic this would be for her, plus being keenly aware that a person is only as sick as his or her secrets, I was encouraged Emily had made the decision to get it all out. Welcoming her determination to be transparent, I told her I had as much time as she required.

Thanking me, Emily began. "I want to get all of this off my chest, except for the way I was sewed up at the hospital. I still can't talk about the scars I received from Bruiser or the barbaric way I was dealt with by that ghoul who treated me."

"I understand," I responded, but I really didn't. I had no idea how difficult this must have been for her, especially since she had been a talented ballerina and successful model. She was the kind of woman who took a great deal of pride in presenting herself with elegance and grace.

Getting straight to the purpose for her call, Emily began. "Not only was what they did to me disfiguring, but it was also soul crushing. Because my husband chose the importance of his relationship with Daren over me, his own wife, something inside of me snapped. My life has never been the same—not since that fateful event—and I don't imagine it ever will be."

I wanted to reassure her that it would, but I knew this would be nothing more than a meaningless promise. I certainly couldn't deliver on such a pledge. Some emotional wounds do last a lifetime and what Emily continued to reveal certainly qualified to be one of them. Nevertheless, learning about what happened did allow me to gain insight into the nature of why

Emily's Jewish faith had become so intense and resilient. It grounded her, providing her with the moral foundation she required to move forward, despite the horrors she had been forced to endure. Additionally, Judaism's moral clarity required her to be straightforward. It provided her with the justification she needed to come forth. Hearing the stories about Epstein's victims on TV was so morally repugnant that she could no longer remain silent.

Going into added detail about what her torture was like in the bungalow, Emily stated. "Eventually, after a particularly hard kick, I ended up on the cold tile floor. I was trapped between the oversized bed and the wall. I was exhausted and in so much pain I stopped fighting. Because I no longer had the ability to protect myself from Bruiser's persistent assault, I just gave up."

"That's when he stopped beating you, right?" I asked, assuming this would be when it ended, but I was wrong.

Correcting my false assumption, Emily said. "No, Jack. That's actually when the intense torture began. I was on the floor stuck between the bed and the thick hurricane proof concrete wall. That's when I saw the flashing blue light on my Blackberry, telling me I had a message. It was all I could look at. I thought that if I could reach it, it might save my life, but it was just beyond my grasp. Having been thrown at me, precisely like Daren threw the slippers at that poor girl, once it hit me, it ended up landing under the bed. Realizing I could not reach it, with all of the pain that I was experiencing, I stopped resisting my husband's attack. It was like I wasn't there anymore."

"I can't even imagine what that must have felt like," I admitted. As disturbed as I was by what I was hearing, I couldn't even finish my comment.

"After being wedged between the bed and the concrete wall, seeing the state I was in, Bruiser wanted to keep me right where I was. To do this, he took his leather belt and twisted it tightly around my left ankle. Then, he secured it to the bed's foot post."

After explaining this, Emily paused for a long moment to regain her composure. Then, she continued. "Keep in mind, when I was thrown out of the SUV, I landed on my right side and bounced. That's how my left thigh was hit midair by the swinging corner of the passenger door."

After another pause, she continued. "It took me three hours to walk to the estate. Much of that time I was actually crawling. Once I was inside the bungalow by about 5:30 a.m., that's when the fight began again."

"How much resistance did you put up?" I asked.

"Not much," Emily admitted. "It was more like Bruiser was punching a rag doll. By that time, I doubt I would have been able to stand. Bruiser pushed, shoved and kicked me into the bedroom. That's when he grabbed my cell phone and threw it at me."

"Being hit by the phone must have hurt?" Jack asked.

"No more than anything else," Emily admitted with a mirthless laugh.

I wondered why she had not used her cell phone to call for help while she was crawling back to Estate Viol, but in my heart I knew. To have done so would have invited further retribution.

Emily continued. "When I was wedged in the corner between the bed and the wall, Bruiser threw himself on top of me—all 250 pounds of him. That knocked the wind out of me. Then he screamed in my face, telling me to 'never ignore him again.' My face was covered with his spit from him screaming. To this day I can still smell it—his foul, rancid spit mixed with Johnny Walker Black. Thinking about that smell still makes me nauseous."

"I can't even imagine," I replied.

"Oh, and I was to never cry," Emily added sardonically. "If I did, 'he would give me something to cry about.' I believed him so I learned not to cry. This was difficult because my natural temperament is to be soft-hearted and emotional. Like so many other things, not being able to cry put me at odds with my true nature."

Becoming philosophical, she added. "This aspect of my punishment was even more painful than being beaten. It was like I was being brainwashed and reprogrammed to be what he wanted me to be. I wasn't allowed to be myself. More than any other thing, this kept me emotionally imprisoned for all of the years we were together. It was so intimidating. It continues to bother me to this day."

"I'm sure," I concurred. "By coming forward, what you are doing will help you regain what you've lost."

"I hope that's true," Emily mused, unconvinced. Returning to her narrative, she added. "With my leg badly bruised, being tied to the bed, my thigh began to turn bluish purple. Because my left foot was losing blood, it also began to turn purple. By this time, most of my body had been beaten so badly that it eventually turned black and blue, but he never hit me in the face. That was off limits. The rest of me was fair game but not my face."

I remembered what she had told me previously, but I didn't interrupt. I knew how significant this conversation would be for her emotional healing. She needed to expel this entire traumatic episode from her system. Doing so was the most cathartic thing she could possibly do. I keenly aware of her need to do it.

"Daren once told Bruiser that I had a beautiful face with flawless coloring. I'm certain this is why Bruiser never struck me in the face. He would never do anything to damage something Daren desired, so he never hit me in the face." After a short pause, she asked. "Can you imagine how infuriating that has been for me to accept?"

"Absolutely! At the same time, I'm glad he didn't, aren't you?"

"Yes, I suppose I am," she replied mirthlessly. "But it's galling at the same time."

Returning to her narrative, she said. "While all of this was happening, Bruiser still had a bottle of Johnny Walker Black in his hand. By this time, it was empty. Having finished it, Bruiser smashed it against the footboard of the bed. When this happened, I thought he was going to cut my throat with the neck of the bottle, but I was wrong."

Having said this, her voice trailed off for a long moment, as she tried to deal with the horror of reliving what happened next. Revealing more than she had earlier, she continued. "He carved up other places instead—places that I have never been willing to show anybody. He cut my vagina open until the broken bottle was too slippery to hold—slippery from my blood."

Again, she stopped. I knew better than to respond or to ask any questions. Instead, I remained quiet and perfectly still waiting for Emily to continue.

A good while later, she did. "This is when Bruiser got scared. I could see it in his face. I watched how his eyes changed from being furious to being fearful. Looking away from me apprehensively, he could see that my blood was slowly making its way under the bed and across the floor to the closet. He could also see a red rivulet of blood begin to flow into the entrance of the bathroom. By this time, although I was still breathing, all resistance had drained from me. I was no longer able to protect myself. I stopped moving. I no longer cared. I was dying. I knew it, so did he. I just didn't care anymore."

Pausing for a long moment to compose herself, Emily sighed. "Seeing me like this created a significant dilemma for Bruiser. He had to do something or I would have died. Grabbing a large black plastic garbage bag from under the kitchen sink, he threw me onto it. He did this so that I would not mess up Daren's new Toyota SUV by bleeding all over it."

When she said this, I noticed her tone changed significantly. Her voice transformed from being mournful to being bitter. That she loathed her husband for what he had done was crystal clear.

"Once I was in the SUV, I was driven to a side entrance of the hospital, not to the ER, not to where there were real doctors and real law enforcement officers. Obviously, this surprised me but it seemed to be a familiar process for Bruiser. At the time, I didn't think much about it, but I certainly did afterwards. I wondered how many other women had suffered the same fate." She stated, almost rhetorically.

"That's what I was wondering too, especially when you told me about where he cut you. He left your face alone, but your vagina was fair game."

"That's right, Jack. By the time we reached the hospital, Bruiser had begun to panic. Although he was genuinely concerned that I might die, I don't believe this was his greatest fear. What scared him more than anything was it would deprive Daren of something he had always wanted but had never experienced."

"Having sex with you," I responded, almost rhetorically.

"That's right. If I died, that would have denied Daren the pleasure of screwing me."

"That's about as twisted as anything I've ever heard," I asserted.

"Isn't it?" Emily mused. "Bruiser told the person attending me, 'Sew her up. Take a goddamn X-ray if you have to but be sure to give it to me.' He even had to control that. 'Fix her,' he demanded. When the man did as he had been paid handsomely to do, I screamed because it was so painful. With no anesthetic whatsoever, that man, whoever he was, sewed me up in a way God never intended for a human being to be put together."

"How horrible that must have been," I admitted. I thought of numerous questions but thought it wiser to allow her to tell her story at her own pace.

"It was," Emily concluded. "So, when I tell you what happened to me, that I am scared to death because of what they still might do to me, I'm not exaggerating or being paranoid. My fear is real and it is legitimate. It is based on an experience that has been so emotionally painful that I have maintained my secrecy about it for nearly fifteen years." Emily continued. "Before we finish, I have one more thing to discuss with you."

"Okay," I replied, wondering what was about to come next.

"The gated community where Estate Viol was located was quite famous on the island. That's because there were several really expensive homes that were owned by celebrities. There was only one road to get there and it was shaped like a horseshoe. At the center of the 'U' was Daren's compound, Estate Viol. On the other side of the U, was the Madras Cotton estate."

After a short pause, she added. "At the end of the cul de sac was Jonathan Bright's estate. He was the author of *Disinformation*. At the other end of the U was one of Dekembe Matuto's estates. He actually had two houses on Saint Thomas." She explained, "Dekembe was a famous Hall of Fame basketball player."

"I know who Dekembe Matuto is," I interrupted with a laugh, affirming my Man Card.

Not paying attention to my disruption, Emily continued. "Just outside of the gated community was Percy Betamann's estate. He's a famous fashion designer from Paris. Do you happen to know who he is?" Emily asked.

"No, I've never heard of him."

"He's very flamboyant. He has really tacky designs for women, but they have made him quite famous."

Knowing better than to ask a question about women's fashion, I wisely refrained.

Moving on, Emily said. "Willie Luckenbach lives on St John, just a few miles away by boat. He's the world famous country singer and songwriter. His home was engulfed by a huge fire and was completely destroyed. He had an infamous one-month marriage to Starla Beau while we lived there. I guess it didn't take Starla long to figure out Willie's preferences. When she did, she had their marriage annulled. Willie was a regular at our restaurant. He would dock his massive yacht at North Drop Point and walk up 120 stairs to dine at our restaurant or get a to-go pizza."

I interrupted. "I get it. There were plenty of important people who frequented the restaurant. I would have suspected this, but why is this important?"

"Because every single celebrity mentioned was invited to or was a regular at one of Daren's famous 'boat parties,'" Emily explained. "Originally, I just thought these were boat parties like people have on Old Hickory Lake or Chickamauga Lake, but I was wrong. I had no idea about the bacchanalia that occurred."

"So, these boat parties involved underage girls?" I asked for clarification.

"Definitely, I was never allowed to attend any of them—just the restaurant's hostesses were invited. Now, I understand why. I was an idiot not to have put it together for so long, but I had no idea what was happening to those girls, other than we could not keep any of them employed as a regular hostess."

Emily added. "This was the perfect setup. Daren would invite guests from the mainland. He would fly them to Saint Thomas on one of his two private planes, along with underage girls. The girls came willingly but soon discovered their presence was to become a sex slave. Some of these girls were brought onto Daren's yacht. It was captained by a man who also knew about everything that was happening on Epstein's 'Orgy Island.'"

"Emily, it's difficult to conceptualize that this level of depravity could exist . . . and that they could get away with sex trafficking, rape and even murder for so long."

"They are still getting away with it, Jack," Emily corrected. "The FBI may have caught up with Jeffrey Epstein, but I don't think Daren Magnus is even on their radar."

"Not yet, he isn't," I corrected. "But we're going to do our best to make sure that changes."

Emily sighed with hopeful anticipation that this might really happen but added nothing else. Shortly thereafter, the conversation ended.

• • •

Once our conversation ended, I turned off the television, which had been muted during our conversation. What I had been watching no longer interested me. I couldn't think of anything other than the events Emily had disclosed. Although I had heard the outline of what happened at our earlier meeting, once I became aware of the magnitude of Emily's brutal attack, it impacted me significantly.

Like Emily, I wondered how Bruiser was aware of where to take her at the hospital. Her husband needed to make certain there would be no record of her being treated. I also wondered how many other girls had suffered a similar fate. Was disfiguring girls standard operating procedure for Bruiser and the others at Estate Viol? I also wondered how many were allowed to live and how many weren't. It probably meant there were victims still alive to tell their tales, if they could be located.

The grotesqueness of my thoughts made me think I had been reading a Bram Stoker or Stephen King novel, but this was real and very disturbing.

Bruiser's rage surprised me. The thought of taking a broken liquor bottle to carve up a woman's vagina was something that very few people would ever consider doing. Not many would even fantasize about engaging in something this vicious and depraved. Such brutality went far beyond the norm of routine domestic violence. To me, it seemed more like Bruiser had a psychotic break, but Emily's husband did remain in enough control to make certain he didn't disfigure her face. There was something about this that also seemed very odd.

Maybe, knowing he couldn't kill her—not and get away with it—meant the assault on Emily was to keep her in line, but the attack just went too far. I couldn't be certain about this. One thing I did know was Bruiser's behavior constituted a crime in all fifty states and in U.S. territories like the Virgin Islands.

The longer I thought about it, the more certain I became that this wasn't the first time Bruiser had done such a thing. If it had been, Bruiser wouldn't have known precisely what to do. He wouldn't have known where to take his wife—the hospital's side entrance—but he did. He also knew exactly whom to contact to tend to her wounds. Finally, he knew whom to pay to keep the authorities from discovering what had happened and how much to pay. Based on each of these things, I concluded that this had happened before, perhaps numerous times before.

Although I did not know it at the time, I have learned that carving up a victim's vagina occurs frequently. For some unfathomable reason unknown to me, sexual predators like Emily's husband enjoy doing this.

Once Bruiser arrived at the side door of the hospital with Emily, there was no dickering about the price that would be paid. Apparently, the sum had previously been established. The man who was about to treat her must have been aware of who Bruiser was. Otherwise, knowing it was illegal, he probably wouldn't have tended to Emily's wounds.

Once the money changed hands, the medical attendant went straight to work. He sewed up Emily. This prevented her from bleeding to death. Not being a real doctor, the man didn't have access to anesthetics, not even topical ones. Because he didn't, Emily wasn't spared the pain from the procedure. She suffered from being stitched up in numerous places without having anything to numb the pain.

Even in battle, this doesn't happen. The first thing a medic does is provide morphine for a wounded soldier, but Emily didn't have this basic medication to help ease her pain. Instead, she was forced to endure another round of torture. This time, it was at the hands of a non-physician—a person who didn't have the training to know what he was doing.

The more I thought about this, the more I believed Emily was fortunate to have survived her assault.

CHAPTER 5

Break Her Longstanding Silence

JULY 2019

As I thought about the viciousness of Emily's attack and how lucky she was to have survived Bruiser's assault with the broken Scotch bottle, I also wondered about how many underage girls had not survived. What about them? What about the horrors they must have endured, suspecting they were about to die? What about the parents of these girls and the daily heartache they have been forced to endure, never knowing for certain what happened to their runaway daughters? Most of all, I wondered how many of them there have been?

As I contemplated each of these questions, I thought about what would be the best and most effective way to speak out for these victims. Of equal importance, I wondered how any of these young girls could be identified? Not having been seen or heard from for the past fifteen years, other than the heartbreak their parents and siblings continued to bear, would anybody in a position of authority even care about them to do anything about it?

Emily didn't know how many there were, not really. All she could do was take a stab at the number but, at best, her guess was no better than an iffy estimate.

But what about the FBI? How would they react when they learned about all of this? Would they take it seriously or not? After the passing of so much time, coupled with not having precise information about the girls involved, would Emily's tale be taken seriously, or would it be sluffed off and never given appropriate consideration? I didn't know. I didn't have the answer to any of these questions. In fact, I didn't have the slightest idea.

It was my intention to contact the Bureau, however, and I planned to do this independently of Emily. My goal was to feel them out about their interest in what I had written, while steadfastly maintaining Emily's anonymity. This was a strategy I thought would work, but I couldn't be certain. The one thing I did know was my intention was to protect Emily. This goal wasn't just wishful thinking. I had a plan about how to make it work.

Because I was the host, along with my brother, of WATTS UP! on BlogTalk Radio for the past ten years, I considered myself to be a journalist—at least in the legal sense. Although I had never obtained press credentials or anything like that, by being a weekly radio talk-show host, I thought it might provide me with sufficient justification to assert my 1st amendment protection of freedom of the press. In this way, I might be able to keep the identity of my confidential informant private.

Although Emily was committed to coming forward, she was equally committed to maintaining her personal protection. As fearful as she had been for the past fifteen years, based on Bruiser's and Daren's intimidation, she needed the assurance of anonymity. It was the only thing that could protect her from being harmed. My plan would provide for this.

At least, this is what I hoped it could do.

Emily was also concerned about the possibility that she might be considered an accomplice to Bruiser's and Daren's criminality. She feared that by not coming forward much sooner, because there are no statute of limitations on murder, this might somehow be held against her.

When she asked me about this, I assured her this wouldn't happen, but I did understand her apprehension. Having written the book, *Betrayal in Charleston*, a true story about Steve Sarkela being kidnapped and tortured by a mobster, I understood the emotional impact post-traumatic stress has on a victim. I knew how debilitating its impact could be. When a person has been traumatized as profoundly as Emily had been, it makes coming forward to confront one's persecutor extremely difficult.

Her post traumatic stress also explained the reason why she was unable to leave Bruiser. As traumatized as she was, she simply couldn't do it. I understood this, but most people wouldn't.

Those who have never had any experience with post-traumatic stress simply can't fathom how difficult it would be for a woman like Emily to leave an abuser like Bruiser, much less to come forward and break her longstanding silence about his criminal activity. Having written Steve Sarkela's book, where post-traumatic stress was a significant factor, I understood this well. Because I did, I knew it was my job to make the FBI understand it as well.

With the arrest of Jeffrey Epstein, I thought the Bureau would be interested in a similar situation that happened in another part of the Virgin Islands. While Epstein was raping girls on Orgy Island, just a few nautical miles away from Estate Viol, Daren Magnus and his friends were doing the same thing—the exact same thing. The only difference was Daren was prudent enough to not get involved with a former President or with British nobility. As clandestine as Jeffrey Epstein was, Daren Magnus was much more so.

Nevertheless, for me to go to the FBI, I needed more detailed information than I had been able to obtain from Emily thus far. I wanted to obtain a specific detailed description about each of the girls, based on Emily's recollection. Just saying there were quite a few and they were probably from the Florida panhandle wasn't nearly enough information for the FBI. I needed the particulars that only Emily could provide, so I asked her, despite knowing her memory was spotty. Perhaps it had even changed somewhat over the years.

When I asked, Emily was immediately forthcoming, but she informed me that her interaction with the restaurant's hostesses was limited.

When I asked why, she replied. "I was not allowed to interact with the hostesses after what I saw that morning . . . not after witnessing that girl's body being taken out of Daren's bedroom."

"But weren't you at the restaurant every day, doing the books and things like that?" I asked.

"Yes, I worked at Fisherman's North Drop," Emily explained, "but after what I had seen, I couldn't keep my mouth shut. I know I should have, but I couldn't. I kept asking questions that neither Bruiser nor Daren wanted to answer. To keep me quiet and to maintain their secrecy about what they were doing, they made the decision to make me leave the restaurant before any of the hostesses arrived for work. That way, I wouldn't know anything about them."

"That's interesting," I replied. "I'll bet you didn't like being kept away one bit."

Emily laughed. "You bet I didn't, but they threatened to lock me in my bungalow again, just like they had done the night I arrived on the day of the 'emergency.' I definitely didn't want that, so I did as I was told."

"I understand. Did they actually threaten locking you up? I mean, literally?"

"You bet they did. I tried to protect those girls. I really did. I even offered to be the hostess at Fisherman's. That way, there would be no need to have any underage hostesses working there."

"How did they receive your offer?"

"My idea was immediately shot down. It was dismissed before I could even finish making the suggestion. Daren said, 'No, we have very special requirements for the hostesses.' He added, 'Nothing personal, Emily, but you are too old.'"

I laughed when he heard this, so did Emily.

Protesting, Emily said. "I was in my thirties. Why would that make me too old to seat people for dinner?"

"I have no idea."

"Later, I thought about what the 'special requirements' actually were." Emily postulated, "What would be necessary to be a hostess at a restaurant? Obviously, I knew precisely what the real requirements were, but I certainly didn't verbalize that."

"I don't blame you."

"They didn't want me around because they didn't want me to start taking the names of the hostesses or to keep any records about what they were doing." She continued, "Because of this, I only have a partial memory of three of the hostesses. There were many others, but I simply don't have any idea who they were. I never got a really good look at many of them, except for a few in passing."

"Well, let's start with the three you know about. Be as specific as you can. It's important."

"I know." Taking a deep breath, she began. "Let me explain the situation as well. Once the restaurant was open and running, we had two steady bartenders. We had a strong wait staff, many of whom had experience working at the Ritz Carlton. It was just down the road from us. Our only employee problem was with the hostesses. They rarely stayed more than two weeks. Some would not even finish their training before they were gone, never to be seen or heard from again."

"I can see why you would have suspicions about what was happening," I interjected. "Tell me about the hostesses you remember."

"The first girl I remember was thin, tall and very young. She was way too young to obtain a server's license. You were required to be eighteen to have one. The girl had dark brown hair, just a little longer than shoulder length. Of all the hostesses, she was the most congenial and the most easygoing. She seemed like a little lost girl. People teased her about being so new to the island. They did this because her skin was very fair. She had absolutely no tan at all."

"That's why she was teased?" I asked.

"Yes, she had very refined features. Rather than wear a skimpy or overly tight dress to work, she wore much better designed clothes." Reflecting, Emily added, "Her wardrobe was much more appropriate than the others."

As Emily was describing the young girl, I was amazed at the detail she provided. Since Emily had been a fashion model, she noticed many things about other women that men simply wouldn't. Although not as helpful as remembering any of the girls' names, I thought this might be useful in reconstructing who these missing victims were after so many years.

Not aware that my thoughts had wondered, Emily continued to describe what she remembered about the first girl. "She was good with makeup and had a natural vibe about her that suited her well. She must have come from a middle or upper middle class family. I detected a slight accent. Perhaps it was Midwestern. There was also a bit of a twang in her voice. Speaking with her once, she apologized for not having a tan by saying that she had not had a chance to go swimming or to lay out by the pool."

Looking intently at me, Emily added, "At the time I wondered what she did during the day if she didn't have enough time to enjoy the pool or the beach. She was easy to talk to though. This made her a good hostess. It meant all of those waiting to be seated in the cramped waiting area had someone pleasant to converse with."

"People had to wait a long time to eat?" I asked. This made me wonder if there were some regulars who might be able to identify any of the young women. Maybe some of the patrons from fifteen years earlier could be located. It was a long shot, but perhaps one of them might come forward with a vital piece of information about one or more of the underage girls.

Emily responded to my question by saying, "No restaurant on the island took reservations, except for a handful. This meant you had to show up and wait if you wanted to eat."

"Business was that good?" I asked.

With a hint of pride in her voice, Emily replied. "We had a first-rate restaurant. Too bad its primary purpose was to provide cover for Daren's depraved sexual activities." Changing gears, she added, "I need to digress for a minute to explain something important."

"Okay."

"The rumor was Daren had purchased a condo at the Ritz Carlton and another at Villa Papillon. The latter is where seasonal college kids stayed, those who came to the island looking for a summer job or for adventure. When I asked Bruiser about the condos, he said he knew of one at the Ritz Carlton that was used for 'Daren's pilots and family.' When my husband said this, I thought, 'How odd.' The estate already had so many bungalows and bedrooms. Why would Daren need more accommodations than we already had?"

Looking at me, she added. "Bruiser's explanation just didn't make sense."

"So, you think this was where Daren housed some of the hostesses? The ones who went missing?"

Emily nodded, "That's exactly what I think."

"You're probably right," I concurred.

"Getting back to the first girl," Emily added. "She only lasted two weeks. The next time I saw her was when those two goons were dragging her out of Daren's bedroom. Seeing her lifeless body like that was horrible." Pausing for a moment, she added, "I will never forget her dress—black floral with sewn in fabric belts flapping in the breeze. The next thing I knew, she was roughly thrown into the back of that SUV."

"I can't imagine witnessing something like that."

"I never saw her again, but I will never forget her either. She was so easy going. She had absolutely no idea how dangerous and deadly the world would prove to be."

Envisioning this girl's brutal demise, I replied. "We are going to get justice for her, Emily. I promise we will." When I stated this, my face had a look of righteous indignation. "One way or another, we will get it." After taking a moment to reflect, I asked. "Is there anything more about her?"

"No."

"Then, what do you remember about the next one?"

With a smile, Emily began. "She was a short, big busted blonde girl who couldn't keep a thought in her head. She would forget everything, unless she wrote it down in her childlike penmanship. She was maybe my height, 5'3", but her boobs must have been store bought. They were huge and did she ever display them, but that's not all. She always wore a top that was way too small. Whether this was on purpose or because she hadn't bought properly sized clothes to fit her figure, I don't know, but she just about popped out of every top she had."

Being a guy, I could easily envision what this girl must have looked like.

"She had foil highlights in her shoulder length hair. She came from money. I could tell that, but it was new money—money that had to flaunt itself. The men loved her of course. She was from Texas and had been a cheerleader. I remember her laughing, saying clichés like, 'The bigger the hair, the closer to God;' and 'The tighter the sweater, the more the boys will like you better.'"

Losing her smile, Emily said. "She had a country laugh and worked for just about one week. Then, she was gone and I never saw her again."

Hearing this, my nostrils flared. Although I wanted to ask if all of these girls were on the restaurant's payroll or were being paid under the table, I didn't. I chose not to distract Emily's train of thought.

"There was a tall, medium built, athletic girl who had her hair braided. She stayed at Villa Papillon. I remember this because she said they had a snack shop right on the beach where she liked to surf and swim. She had a tan and strong athletic shoulders, probably because of how much she liked to swim. Her nails were painted, but she picked at them all the time. So, the polish was chipped and worn off. She had a distinct New England accent. Not Bostonian like the Kennedys, but definitely New England. Maybe she was from Maine or New Hampshire."

Having grown up in Newton, Massachusetts, I knew the difference between the way northern New Englanders spoke and the way Bostonians spoke. It was significant.

Emily couldn't remember the names of any of the girls, but she did remember some very specific aspects about several of them. "I remember asking the New Englander about her braids. The young girl said, 'Yeah, I got them done down in Charlotte Amalie at one of the street vendors cause it was cheap.' She said that Saint Thomas was the farthest she had ever been from home but added, 'it wasn't far enough.'"

When I heard this, I wasn't surprised. I suspected that none of these runaway girls would have put themselves in harm's way if they had had a better home environment. I doubted they would ever have taken off to a Caribbean island without telling someone either, not if they had grown up in a more-stable situation. Unfortunately, each ended up jumping from the proverbial frying pan into the fire.

Referring to the girl from upper New England, Emily said. "She bought her dresses from street vendors. One dress was black but the fabric was so thin it was nearly see-through. It tied behind her neck, showing off her shoulders. I think she had a tattoo on her neck and back—not a huge one but big enough to notice. Her ears were pierced multiple times, with a cartilage piercing. She said she was a beach bum and was disappointed in Saint Thomas because its beaches were so small. She said the best beach was at the Ritz, which I found interesting. That really stayed with me. I wondered how a beach bum, who was so broke she got her hair and clothes from street vendors, could afford to stay at the Ritz? There was no way she would have passed the dress code or the hair code to get a job at the Ritz. They were known on the island for being extremely strict. That girl was only at our restaurant for one week. That meant we had three hostesses in one month."

"And that was just the first month?" I asked.

"That's right," Emily agreed. "After that, I was kept away from the hostesses. That's why I don't really know how many more of them there were. I was told I was interfering with restaurant business by talking to the girls. Not one of them ever complained or seemed unhappy being a hostess. Yet they would 'leave' and be replaced with ease. It was as if there was a waiting list to work as a hostess at Fisherman's North Drop."

"Can you think of anything else?" I asked.

"Well, I noticed that a hostess type was evolving. Each girl, with just a few exceptions, was 5'7" or taller, had long blonde or medium blonde hair, was thin and wore clothes that were too tight. I suspect they were required to wear the clothes they did. The dresses always seemed to be some variation of black. The skirts were revealing and their halter tops didn't halt much."

When I heard this, I laughed out loud. I couldn't help himself. Replaying the halter top line in my mind several times, I made a mental note to use it in one of my Moon Series novels.

Emily concluded the conversation by saying, "Not one of these girls was old enough to serve liquor. There was also a certain naiveté about each of them, but that was as much specific information as I could ascertain. From that point forward, I was 'forbidden' from going to the restaurant unless Daren invited me himself."

"It's obvious they didn't want you around."

Looking at me, Emily asked an important question. "Do you think any of this will help, or is it too sketchy?"

"I do believe it will help, especially where parents are concerned. If I had a daughter who had been missing for fifteen years, I would be able to recognize her by the descriptions you've given. You pinpointed the personality types of all three very well. That's a big deal."

Smiling, Emily's shoulders sagged. She wanted to be helpful. "I wish I could remember their names. I've tried to remember a thousand times, but I always come up blank."

"You've remembered a lot," I affirmed once again. Suspecting our time together was drawing to a close, I asked. "Is there anything else you want to add."

"Yes, and what I have to say is very important," Emily replied immediately.

"Okay, let's hear it," I replied, somewhat startled.

"It's about Daren's motivation for all of this. His goal was to promote Fisherman's North Drop to all of the Economic Development Corporations, the EDCs. The men who ran these fraudulent corporations were required to live on the island for a minimum of 186 days a year."

For Daren's EDC, Viol Enterprises, Emily was the person originally chosen to spend that amount of time on the island, but this arrangement didn't last long.

"These wealthy tax cheats sheltered their money in the Virgin Islands to defraud the IRS," she affirmed. "All of them were uber wealthy and older. Daren was the youngest and he liked it that way. This was a distinction he coveted."

"That doesn't surprise me. It seems very much in character for his narcissistic personality," I replied.

Emily concurred. "Daren even developed the restaurant's menu to suit the tastes of this group of EDCs."

Noticing how intrigued I was by this, Emily continued. "Looking back, it was more than the menu that was developed specifically to suit the tastes of these men. The hostesses, the underage girls who were paraded before them, were the real menu item. When these EDCs were making their food selections, I believe they were actually making their entertainment selection for the night as well."

"What!" I exclaimed, nearly coming out of my seat. Despite having heard so much about what happened on Saint Thomas, this revelation rattled me. In my wildest dreams, I could never have imagined such depravity, but it was all being paraded in plain sight for the pleasure and enticement of lecherous pedophiles at a fancy restaurant. The other patrons, the non-predators, were completely oblivious. They had no idea what was happening to these underage hostesses.

"It's horrible, isn't it?"

"Yes, it is," I concurred emphatically.

"I really do believe this was what was happening. It was like a real-life double entendre being played out in plain sight, with only Daren and his fellow-pedophiles understanding what was truly happening. This is what made it so deliciously wicked for them. It was soul-satisfying for Daren—Bruiser too." Looking at me, Emily added scornfully. "The food was just an hor d'oeuvre. The real entrée was the hostess."

When I heard this, another aspect of Daren's sex trafficking operation clicked into place. I understood why Daren needed the additional housing at the Ritz and at Papillon. The Ritz was an elegant place where the mighty EDCs would be able to enjoy their sumptuous carnal feasting in style.

Changing direction, Emily said. "One night, when we were all dining together, which was very rare, I asked Daren what his next project was going to be. By this time, Estate Viol had been completely renovated and redecorated. The restaurant was open and had become a roaring success. His answer shocked me. He said he had run into 'this guy at the airport who told him to buy an island.' The guy said Daren should 'forget about Saint Thomas. Just use the airport's runway.' The man added, 'If you want real privacy, buy an island of your own.'"

When I heard this, my ears perked up. "Do you think Daren was alluding to Jeffrey Epstein?"

"That's exactly what I think. Daren didn't name him, but I always knew who he was talking about when he referred to the 'gray-haired dude.'" She continued. " Fisherman's overlooked the Little Brass Islands and one of them was supposedly for sale. We could actually see the island from the patio at Estate Viol. It was that close. I asked Daren if he was serious about this and he replied, 'You're goddamn right, I am. It just depends on how much it will cost to build what I need.' Looking at me, he asked, 'Can you imagine the view? Can you imagine the privacy?'"

"Daren was planning to replicate what Epstein had created, mimicking it to a tee, wasn't he?"

"That's precisely what Daren had in mind. He wanted an Orgy Island of his own. My mouth must have hung open from shock, when I learned about his plan."

"Mine certainly would have," I agreed.

"At the time, I wondered why Daren would need that much privacy, but I knew the answer. I was just unwilling to admit it to myself. In addition to the secrecy, having his own island was a way for Daren to keep up with the other men in the 'Three Commas Club.'"

"The what?"

"The Three Commas Club."

"What in the hell is the Three Commas Club!?" I asked, somewhat confused.

"It's a club for billionaires. To be a member, you have to have three commas in your net worth," she explained.

Working out what this meant, I asked, "By having three commas, this meant you were a billionaire, right?"

"Correct."

"Is that a real thing?" I asked incredulously.

"Yes, the Three Commas Club was a very real thing, at least back in 2004 and 2005. I don't have any idea if it still exists or not."

Further delving into an explanation about Daren's motivation to have his own private island just like Epstein's, Emily explained. "Daren was super competitive. Back then, he was in full Three Commas Club mode. Daren wanted to prove his commas to everyone." Looking at me with a smile, she added. "And there's nothing like having your own private island to do just that. Daren thought it would prove him worthy of being a member in the Three Commas Club."

"There's nothing worthy about any of this, Emily."

"I know. It's so perverse."

As indignant as I had ever been in my entire life, I concluded. "It should have been called the Three Commas of Depravity." Looking off for a long moment, I added. "I can't wait to tell the FBI about this; I really can't."

"The first time I heard about it, I was horrified," Emily admitted.

Truly offended by the degeneracy of these men, I added. "The arrogance and gall of these super-entitled billionaires. Because of 'who they were,' in their inflated view of themselves, they somehow justified raping, killing and discarding runaway girls just because they had the power to do it. Who in the hell do they think they are?"

"Jack, when they would sit at the bar at Fisherman's, they would brag about achieving their third comma. Most people had no idea what these EDC tax cheats were talking about, but I did." Emily added, "They bragged about other things too."

"Like what?"

"Like calling themselves 'whales.' It was code for having had sex with an underage girl."

Hearing this, my mouth actually dropped open. That anybody would take pride in such degeneracy was deeply offensive.

"Each of these men considered himself to be a whale. 'The gray-haired dude' was the supreme whale," she added. "He was revered by all of them."

"Jeffrey Epstein, the 'gray-haired dude,'" I mocked scornfully.

"Yes. They admired him because he had gotten away with it for so long. As far as I can tell, all of the EDCs in the Three Commas Club have been getting away with it for years, some for decades," Emily added.

"Well, hopefully not anymore. We're going to do everything we can to put a stop to this and give these victimized girls a voice."

Hearing this, Emily felt good about having confided in me. Seeing this happen was a goal she also desired.

CHAPTER 6

He Had a Large Carving Knife

NOVEMBER 2006

By Thanksgiving in 2006, if it had been Bruiser's purpose to intimidate Emily to the point where he would be completely confident she would never consider opening her mouth about Daren's sex trafficking, or be a threat to either of them in any way, then he had been completely successful. Emily's near death experience from having her vagina cut open with a broken bottle of Johnny Walker Black had completely cowed her into submission, at least outwardly. It wasn't that she had been beaten into compliance as much as she had been traumatized into remaining silent.

This is what post-traumatic stress does. It keeps a person bottled up. There was another aspect to Emily's commitment to maintain silence. Within the deepest recesses of her heart, she was certain her husband was deeply involved in Daren Magnus's criminal enterprise. Despite this, like so many other battered women, she continued to minimize and excuse her husband's role in what was happening. Her own mental well-being required her to make rationalizations for his behavior, despite how implausible they were.

Because they were married, a union that made her his partner in life, she consistently gave her husband the benefit of the doubt, denying he was as deeply involved in sex trafficking as he must have been—perhaps murder as well.

To maintain her sanity and her sense of wellbeing, she had to do this. At least, she believed she had no other choice. Since a spouse cannot testify against her husband, she actually believed her survival—her very life depended upon her continuing to be an obedient, submissive wife. This included keeping her mouth shut.

Since Daren hadn't achieved his goal of becoming intimate with Emily, this also acted as an insurance policy for her. In her heart, she knew having sex with Daren would never happen, but he certainly didn't. That he continued to look forward to bedding Emily worked in her favor, and she wanted to keep it that way.

Being as feisty and principled as she was, however, taking a mental health holiday from reality proved to be very difficult. Although she and Bruiser quarreled about many things, they never argued about what was really bothering her. That subject, the subject of what happened to the underage hostess who simply disappeared, remained a verboten topic of conversation.

As close as Emily came to succumbing to her injuries the night Bruiser carved her up, how could anyone blame her for remaining silent about what happened? How could she be chastised for doing everything she could to simply stay alive? In her mind, she had no alternative course of action other than the one she chose—not and remain among the living.

Her willingness to provide her husband with a pass for his unhealthy relationship with Daren Magnus continued for about a year, but then it ended abruptly. When it did, it was like the crash of Humpty Dumpty. Once her fragile world that was being held together by deception and willful avoidance of reality was irreversibly broken, there was nothing that could put it back together again. An event occurred at Fisherman's that revealed the darkness in her husband, completely exposing his depravity to the light of day.

The chef at the restaurant happened to be from the Culinary Institute of America. The Institute playfully referred to itself as the CIA. His name was Fabio Silva and he was the chef at Fisherman's North Drop, a very good chef by the way. His cuisine was excellent, making the restaurant a very popular spot on the island. Fabio was a short, kind and gregarious Brazilian. Always smiling, in addition to being a great chef, he was also a decent human being.

One afternoon, while Fabio was in the kitchen preparing for the evening crowd, he heard Bruiser become verbally abusive to Emily. The argument between the couple quickly escalated, becoming a verbal assault against her that Fabio suspected might end up being a physical altercation. Thinking he had no alternative other than to intervene, Fabio made a decision to confront Bruiser.

By the time he did, Emily had run into the ladies' room and locked the door behind her. Fearful that Bruiser might hurt her like he had done previously, especially since he had already consumed a couple of drinks, she refused to come out. While he was beating on the restroom door, demanding that she open it, Fabio approached him.

The chef, who had bolted through the kitchen quickly and purposefully, was very angry. He had a large carving knife in his hand. In no uncertain terms, he told Bruiser to stop harassing Emily, but that's not all. He directed Bruiser to leave the restaurant immediately. Giving the startled man a way to extricate himself without losing face, Fabio directed Bruiser to pick up some supplemental supplies at the East End of the island.

Realizing he didn't want the confrontation to escalate or to continue making a public spectacle out of himself, Bruiser prudently abandoned his quarrel with Emily, got in his white Forerunner and left to retrieve the groceries. An additional part of his motivation to leave was Bruiser didn't want the chef to inform Daren that he had been behaving inappropriately at the restaurant.

Bully that he was, Bruiser was used to getting his way, but Fabio was not a helpless woman. Because he was a formidable man who knew what he was doing with a knife, Bruiser chose to retreat as discretely as possible.

Once Bruiser drove off, Fabio knocked on the ladies' room door gently, telling Emily that it was safe to come out. He also told her the entire kitchen staff had heard the commotion and were willing to come to her defense. They liked her but none of them liked Bruiser, not even a little.

Although Emily was grateful for the support, she was deeply humiliated that her dark secret about Bruiser's temper was becoming widely known. Although public awareness of his violent nature was the one thing that might keep her safe, it was the last thing she wanted people to know. Like many battered women, as ironic and incongruous as it might seem, Emily was as deeply invested in keeping her situation a secret as she was in ensuring her survival.

Once Emily exited the ladies' room, Fabio took her by the hand, led her to a table in the restaurant and asked her to sit down. Excusing himself, he told her he needed to show her something and would return with it quickly.

A minute later, Fabio reappeared with several baseball hats with the restaurant's name on them. Seeing them, Emily couldn't imagine why a formal restaurant such as Fisherman's North Drop had invested in such a low class item as a cap. Explaining how this came about, Fabio informed Emily that while she was back on the mainland, where she had been directed to stay for an extended period, despite being required to be on the island for half a year, Daren had custom ordered the hats. They were for him and some of his closest friends. While dining at the restaurant, the hats were given to select patrons—those who had been invited to attend Daren's special parties.

Looking uncomfortable, Fabio handed several of the hats to Emily, while simultaneously apologizing for being the one required to tell her what their true purpose was.

Taking the hats, Emily saw what was emblazoned on them. On the front, the hats read, "Crotch Cannibal." On the back, it read, "Eat Til It Bleeds."

Seeing this, although shaken from her latest explosive episode with Bruiser, Emily was appalled and horrified. A moment later, her stomach lurched. Overcome by disturbing emotions, she started to cry and couldn't stop.

Fabio, who understood how devastating this must have been for her, sat patiently, patting her hand supportively.

Seeing the hats for herself, Emily could no longer maintain any semblance of self-delusion. She had to admit her husband was deeply involved in Daren's sex trafficking. She had the proof of what she had long denied in her hands. Worst of all, the entire staff at the restaurant knew what she had been trying to conceal. Fisherman's North Drop was just a cover to camouflage Daren Magnus's sex trafficking operation for the whales of The Three Commas Club. That it was successful and made money was incidental.

Looking at the back of one of the hats reminded her of what Daren had once said to her. "I like to hurt it." Remembering what "it" referred to made her stomach lurch again.

Daren liked to hurt a female's vagina. This was his true aphrodisiac. He wasn't content to just destroy a young girl's life by robbing her of her innocence, he also had to inflict pain on her in the process, going so far as to kill at least one of them.

Seeing the hat, Emily's mind flashed back to what happened that Saturday morning, when the "cleaners" removed the body of the restaurant's hostess. The previous evening, the "Crotch Cannibal" had gone too far. He had killed the girl. Unremorseful for what he had done, he threw her shoes at her in anger. Finally grasping the depth of her boss's aberrant nature, she could no longer squelch her need to vomit. Racing to the restroom, she arrived just in time.

CHAPTER 7

No Evidence of Disease

2002

Clearly, Emily's marriage to Bruiser was a nightmare and had been for a long time. This seems obvious to anyone, which begs the question. Why would she put up with such blatant abuse and criminal behavior? Why didn't she just leave?

After reading about Bruiser's violent attack, the natural question any right-minded person would ask is why didn't Emily simply pack up her belongings and move away? Nobody could possibly have faulted her for doing so. One could even make the argument that Emily must have had a screw loose to stay with Bruiser as long as she did.

Leaving might seem like the obvious solution to Emily's ongoing problem with being physically assaulted, but the resolution to her marital problems wasn't as easy or as simple as it appears to be on the surface. Real life, despite our desire to make it trouble-free, is nearly always complicated. Emily's life was obviously no exception.

It was filled with nuances and conflicting motivations that made simple answers to complex problems extraordinarily difficult. If Emily had left Bruiser, which she considered routinely, she was convinced departing would put her life in danger. Given her experience, this conclusion seemed justifiable. Additionally, because she had no access to funds of her own and few marketable skills, she felt stuck.

Because a wife cannot be compelled to testify against her husband, she reasoned that remaining married was her best insurance policy to continue living her financially comfortable but miserable life. She maintained this belief, while simultaneously knowing that by continuing to live with him, she was putting her life in harm's way each and every day. She understood that, in his rage, Bruiser might become so out of control that he would inadvertently kill her. She constantly feared being beaten to death, either intentionally or unintentionally.

Her situation created a dilemma with significant conflicting variables, but her quandary had other aspects to it as well. Having been married to Bruiser for more than a dozen years, she had a huge investment in his life. This included the potential to be financially set for life based on Bruiser's association with Daren Magnus. Being prosperous was very appealing to Emily.

With both her husband and Daren being an integral part of every aspect of her life, including how she made a living, she was clearly hesitant about walking away from her source of financial security. She knew that if she left Bruiser, he would do everything in his power to make certain she didn't receive a fair settlement. His goal would be to leave her penniless, just like Daren had done when his wife divorced him. Daren said that he wanted his ex-wife's financial situation to hurt so bad that "even her grandparents would feel the pain."

Emily felt certain Bruiser would treat her just as unfairly. It was in his nature to do so, but there was another piece to this puzzle that made it difficult for her to just pick up and leave.

She genuinely loved her husband when she married him. Most women do, but there was more to it than this. The couple shared a significant life-altering experience that bound them together tightly. At least, it did for her.

Bruiser had a near death experience that connected the two of them in ways that only those who have had similar experiences can fully appreciate. Shortly before Bruiser met Daren, Emily's husband nearly died from cancer. This happened not long after they were married in 1998. Bruiser and Emily had just bought a house in Rutherford County. Their home was located about twenty miles southeast of Nashville.

During their first year in the house, like so many other young couples, they spent a great deal of time, energy and money upgrading their home. It was a wonderful time for both of them. During this period, Bruiser worked as a contractor for the Southern Company. It was a good job that he enjoyed. Although he was paid by the hour, Bruiser made a good living.

Life was pleasant for the Chambers. Because Bruiser had not yet turned into the bully he would become, Emily was very happy with the decision she had made to marry him.

Bruiser was very proud about his appearance. An essential ingredient to look good was for him to always be well tanned. Because this was so important, he purchased his own tanning bed so that he could stay very dark year round.

After using it for quite a while, Bruiser complained that his back was often itchy. Nearly every time Emily turned to look his way, she noticed her husband was scratching the upper right side of his back against the corner of a wall. He did this so frequently that Emily finally became concerned. Telling him to take his shirt off so that she could take a good look at what was causing the itch, she spotted a new mole. It was about the size of a pencil eraser. It was jet black, located under his right shoulder blade.

Horrified by what she saw, the following morning Emily made an appointment for her husband to see a dermatologist. As vain as Bruiser was, he wasn't really concerned about the mole, but he did want it to be removed. Since it was a blemish, this was an unacceptable flaw in his appearance, so Bruiser didn't balk about seeing a doctor.

Emily, who was far more realistic about what the blemish might mean, realized this mole might be something far more serious than an unsightly growth that required removal.

At the appointment, the dermatologist said that because of its location, the mole was most likely a reaction to laundry detergent. Not considering it to be anything serious, she cut the mole off with a scalpel. During the appointment, the dermatologist mentioned that she had lost her husband to melanoma. When Emily heard this, her insides froze. She suspected her husband might have the same problem.

The doctor never considered this to be possible, however. Instead, she consistently maintained that it was nothing more than an allergic reaction to soap. This satisfied Bruiser but not Emily.

Nearly a week later, on Feb 22, 2002, the doctor placed a conference call to all three of them with the pathology report. Both Bruiser and Emily were on the phone but in separate locations. He was at his office, while she was on their home phone.

After greeting the two, the first thing the doctor said was, "I am so sorry. The pathology report has come back and Bruiser does have melanoma."

When Emily heard this, her knees buckled. Alone in their Rutherford County condo, she staggered to a chair to keep from falling. Bruiser's response, unlike Emily's, was to be nonplussed. He didn't seem to be bothered by the pathology report in the least.

Discussing what Bruiser's next steps needed to be, the dermatologist told them they needed to make an appointment with a surgical oncologist immediately. She also apologized to Bruiser for shaving his mole, rather than doing a punch biopsy. Because of the technique she used, the pathologist could not accurately stage Bruiser's melanoma—not since the mole had been cut in half. The dermatologist also stated that Bruiser needed to be seen by a hematologist oncologist to begin a treatment plan. After apologizing a final time, the penitent dermatologist hung up. When she did, Bruiser and Emily were free to discuss the situation.

Responding to what he had just heard, Bruiser said. "I guess I'll have to have surgery, but it's just skin cancer. All they need to do is cut it out."

Hearing her husband's cavalier reaction to his diagnosis, Emily couldn't believe how ludicrous his thinking was. Could he be in complete denial, she wondered, or was he really this uninformed about how serious melanoma could be? She didn't know.

As she sat at their kitchen table for a long time, her heart ached for what was ahead of them, especially for the suffering her husband was about to experience. She knew melanoma was not a minor issue. Bruiser may have been thickheaded about what the dermatologist said, but Emily certainly was not. She was well aware of exactly how deadly melanoma could be.

Continuing to take charge of Bruiser's health care, Emily set up an appointment for him with a surgeon the following day. At the appointment, the surgeon explained everything about the necessary procedures awaiting Bruiser, as well as the surgery that was required to save Bruiser's life. Listening, Emily's husband seemed concerned, but he didn't appear to be worried about the outcome.

During the treatment that followed, the doctor used a dye to determine if the melanoma had spread to Bruiser's lymph nodes. They needed to establish clear margins. Knowing how important this was, Emily was an emotional wreck. She didn't want to be a widow at such a young age. Besides, at this point, her husband was still being nicer to her than he was being abusive. Not wanting to lose him, Emily's bond with Bruiser tightened, deepened and strengthened considerably.

When such a solid connection is established, like it had been for Emily during this crisis, it became an attachment that could not be easily broken. More than any other factor, this was why Emily remained with Bruiser long after most women would have either left him or had him arrested for domestic violence—a fate he definitely deserved.

Because she nearly lost him at such an early age, more than any other factor, this is what continued to bind Emily to Bruiser far beyond the time when she should have left.

Shortly thereafter, Bruiser had his surgery. The doctor removed his skin down to his shoulder blade. The surgery also required twenty-two lymph nodes to be removed. Before Emily could see him after his surgery, the surgeon took her aside to a quiet room. He tried to prepare her for what Bruiser would look like after the operation. This included a lengthy description about the drains that required insertion. Before the surgeon left, he said he had hoped to have "clear margins," but he wasn't certain that he had. This scared Emily more than anything else the doctor told her. It meant their nightmare might need to be replicated.

When they rolled Bruiser out of recovery, he had changed considerably. Looking at him, he seemed so different that Emily didn't think he even looked like her husband. She felt like crying but she didn't. She would not allow herself to be weak. Besides, she didn't want him to think he was being rejected by her in any way.

Bruiser ended up requiring two more surgeries to obtain the clear margins that were required to ensure his long-term survival. Like the first, each of the subsequent surgeries was painful and difficult. Nevertheless, Emily, always the trooper, remained steadfast in her support for her husband. Having promised to love him in sickness and in health, she remained true to her word. She stood beside him supportively throughout every step of his prolonged ordeal.

The entire process deepened her commitment to Bruiser considerably, but it didn't have a reciprocal effect. Essentially, there was no sense of mutuality—not for Bruiser. Because the surgery concerned him and not her, he lacked empathy, appreciation and even awareness about what Emily was going through to be supportive. In his self-centeredness, it probably never occurred to him that his ordeal was nearly as difficult for her as it was for him. This aspect of his nature, being empathetic, was either stunted or it didn't exist.

When a couple is required to face a life-altering crisis like the Chambers had just been through, it usually draws them closer together or it drives them further apart—one or the other. Neither of these outcomes was what they experienced. Theirs was a hybrid. While Emily drew closer to Bruiser, he focused exclusively on himself. Because he did, he drifted further away from her. The net effect resulted in the emotionally toxic relationship that solidified between them. Its toxicity eventually became so pronounced that it deteriorated into a physically dangerous situation for Emily.

Once the three surgeries were completed, there was a debate between the doctors about whether Bruiser was in stage 2B or stage 3A of melanoma. The difference between the two could not have been more profound. If Bruiser had been in stage 3A, his life expectancy would have been no longer than three-to-five years. If he was in stage 2, with treatment, he could eventually become a NED. This is an acronym for a patient who displays "No Evidence of Disease." Obviously, this was a much more desirable prognosis that the alternative.

As part of Bruiser's recovery, he required an MRI with dye injected into him every six months. Chemotherapy was also part of his protocol but, because he would lose his hair, Bruiser refused to submit to it.

To make things easier for his recovery, the couple decided they needed a home that had the master bedroom on the main floor. So, they bought a home that was owned by the famous author, Casey Ward. She had purchased it for her brother but, once her brother had several children, the family outgrew the home. When Bruiser and Emily closed on the property, Casey actually gave them a signed copy of one of her first books, *Now I Lei Me Down to Sleep*.

The first night in their new home at Squash, Bruiser told Emily that if he died, he wanted her to be in a "good house in a really good neighborhood." To her recollection, this was the last genuinely kind and caring comment he ever made. It meant a great deal at the time.

Having lost every home she had ever lived in during her childhood, mostly through foreclosure, she wanted this to be her forever house. She wanted it to be the one where she would live with her loving husband for the rest of their lives. This was her dream and her cherished goal, but it certainly would not be her reality.

THE THREE COMMAS CLUB

CHAPTER 8

Fishing Without a License

2007

That Emily was dedicated to her marriage was clear. It could be seen by her steadfast commitment to honor her wedding vows. She had promised to love Bruiser in sickness and in health, and this is exactly what she did. To do anything less would never have entered her mind. Being a faithful woman was part of her well-established Jewish value system.

Being principled, she not only took her faith seriously, but she was also constitutionally incapable of behaving otherwise. Nevertheless, this wasn't the only reason she remained with her husband, even after he became abusive.

Although never a genuinely kind man, Bruiser's mean-streak became more pronounced once he became involved with Daren Magnus. Although the mentoring Bruiser received created a financial windfall for the Chambers, it came with a terrible price tag. Everything about Daren's life was shady and devious, and this rubbed off on Bruiser easily.

Like many women, Emily greatly desired financial security. To obtain it and to enjoy the lifestyle it produced, she chose to engage in what Daren and Bruiser were doing. She did this on a limited scale, even though she remained in the dark about most of their perversions for quite a while.

For example, five years after Bruiser's near-death experience with melanoma, Daren had the opportunity to purchase two more Harley dealerships. The problem was the "Motorcompany," as it was known to the owners of Harley dealerships, would only permit three dealerships per owner. Additionally, each dealership was allowed to have a small satellite.

The satellite for Daren's Knoxville dealership was in Wilton Springs. This satellite became wildly successful. In fact, it became too successful to continue being considered a satellite. Because it was slated to become its own stand-alone dealership, this created a problem for Daren. He wanted to buy the Jackson and Cocke County Harley dealerships but, with the Wilton Springs store about to outgrow its satellite status, this meant Daren would own four dealerships, one more than the Motorcompany would allow.

To circumvent this limitation, Daren created an umbrella holding corporation to have control over all of his dealerships. To make this work, Daren decided to make Bruiser an offer. In name only, Bruiser would become the owner of both the Jackson and Cocke County Harley dealerships. As his reward, Bruiser would be given a small percentage of each. All that was required was for him to complete the Motorcompany application and pass a background check.

Bruiser was thrilled with this offer and celebrated like a child who had just received a coveted toy from Santa. Not long afterwards, when Bruiser learned about the extent of the background check, his elation evaporated. Troubled, he finally came to Emily and admitted that he would not pass the background check.

Hearing this, Emily was taken aback. "Why not?" She asked.

Reluctantly, Bruiser admitted, "Because I have been arrested and put in jail."

Hearing this made Emily feel sick. By this point, they had been married for more than ten years. Nevertheless, this was the first she had heard about her husband having been incarcerated.

Being direct, Emily asked him. "What were you arrested for?"

With a perfectly straight face, Bruiser responded. "For fishing without a license."

Although he had mentioned this to her earlier in their marriage, she had forgotten it. Emily's intuition, however, told her Bruiser's answer might be less than forthcoming. Despite this, she didn't choose to challenge his truthfulness. Instead, she said that because the arrest was for something so trivial neither Daren nor the Motorcompany would reject his application because of it. It was just too inconsequential.

Emily's assurance should have satisfied Bruiser, but it didn't. His negative, hostile and frosty reaction told her everything she needed to know. His arrest had been for something more significant than fishing without a license. Emily felt certain she would soon discover what he had really done. When she did, whatever secret Bruiser was hiding would be exposed.

Later that day, Bruiser called Daren to tell him the same idiotic story he had told her.

Without questioning anything concerning the specifics of Bruiser's story, Daren responded. "That won't be a problem. I will just make Emily the principal owner instead of you."

Hearing this, Emily was stunned, but she was also pleased. It would give her status and a chip in the game. Being the owner would also enhance her marital situation substantially.

Bruiser was equally shocked, but he certainly wasn't pleased, quite the contrary. With the phone still in his hand, he turned to Emily, who was on the extension. He looked at her with a glare of pure malice. Despite his obvious displeasure with her, Bruiser hypocritically remained cheerful and supportive about the idea to Daren.

Having made his decision, Daren promptly sent the application to Emily, making certain to copy Bruiser on the email. Not in the least fooled by Bruiser's positive response to being replaced by Emily, Daren intended to twist the knife into his underling's jealous heart, knowing that putting Emily's name on the application and not his would be intimidating and infuriating.

Dutifully, Emily completed the application and signed it. She also gave her permission for the Motorcompany to perform a background check on her.

In his childish insecurity, Bruiser let Emily know he would be the one running the dealerships and making all decisions, not her. To reassert himself as master of his domain, he also called Daren to inform him about what Emily's role would be.

Not in the least intimidated, Daren refused to assuage Bruiser's wounded ego in any way. Instead, Daren said, "We'll see who will be the GM." Without further ado, he promptly hung up the phone on his subordinate.

• • •

Several days later, Bruiser returned to their Squash home in the middle of the afternoon, which was unusual. He never arrived early. He did this because Daren told him to return home and put Emily on the extension for a conference call. Once they connected, Daren said he had performed his own independent background check on Bruiser.

Enjoying himself immensely, Daren added. "I did this just for fun." Upon saying this, Daren began to read what the background report revealed. By the tone in his voice, it was clear Daren was thrilled to be the bearer of bad tidings.

Bruiser, who was listening on the main line so that Emily could watch his reactions from the other room, wasn't enjoying himself, not in the least. He looked like a trapped animal. Based on what Daren was disclosing, Bruiser had been arrested many times.

One of the arrests was for fishing without a license just like Bruiser said, but there were numerous other arrests as well. He had been arrested for trespassing and for being a Peeping Tom. He had been incarcerated for that crime multiple times in several counties in Tennessee.

Horrified by what was being revealed about the man she slept with every night, Emily realized she had been "one flesh" in a marriage to a sexual deviant since day one. His aberrant behavior wasn't new. He had been like this all along. Emily was simply unaware of it, but now she was.

Just the thought of having been intimate with a man like this for over a decade sickened her, but it really shouldn't have. After all, by this time she had become aware of what was happening at Estate Viol. Despite this, hearing her husband's past, as it was being read verbatim from police records, meant she could no longer maintain her illusion that their marriage would eventually stabilize and become everything she had ever dreamed it would be. Equally as disturbing, she suspected this might also jeopardize her economic security.

Hiding her physical and emotional scars masterfully, she maintained the illusion to the outside world that the Chambers were a happy couple.

As difficult to accept as what Daren had already read, he wasn't nearly finished with his litany of crimes. He had saved the best for last. He announced that Bruiser had committed bank robbery and embezzlement.

Hearing this, she realized her husband wasn't just a pervert. He was also a thief. Emily, who had had no previous knowledge about Bruiser's criminal past, other than fishing without a license, was floored.

In his younger days, Bruiser had been a bank teller. In this capacity, he had taken cash from his drawer on several occasions. Learning about this for the first time, Emily was dumbfounded. This was the last straw for her. Their marriage was finally over. She no longer felt the need to be tied to him. The emotional bonds were broken. All that remained between them was their lucrative business arrangement.

What she had just heard, coupled with what she already knew, was beyond her capacity to accept, rationalize or forgive. Bruiser had been deceiving her for a decade. Acknowledging the unvarnished truth about who her husband really was in their long, tumultuous marriage, Emily admitted to herself that she was legally bound to a bank embezzling, wife beating, Peeping Tom.

As disgusted as this made her, she was also furious—not just with him but also with herself. Now, instead of owning two dealerships to help her husband become more successful, she intended to use this arrangement as leverage over him. Although not proud of herself for being manipulative, she fully intended to play out the hand she had been dealt.

At that precise moment, she stopped loving Bruiser. This criminal had beaten her caring nature completely out of her. Although it had taken Emily much too long to come to this point, once she reached it, there would be no turning back. She was done and she knew it. Silently, all of this transpired within Emily's heart, while Daren continued to read additional instances of Bruiser's extensive criminal record. It was a long rap sheet.

Thoroughly enjoying himself, Daren taunted Bruiser for no reason other than he could. Since this was an assault to Bruiser's fragile ego, a humiliation he could not tolerate, he insisted that Daren perform a background check on Emily as well.

Bruiser maintained that Emily wasn't "worthy of being the principal owner of a Harley dealership."

Laughing contemptuously, Daren said he had already performed Emily's background check. "Unlike you," Daren replied snidely, "Emily is squeaky clean."

Being rebuked and humiliated, Bruiser turned his head and looked at Emily with hateful black eyes. They bore a hole right through her, scaring her to nearly becoming incontinent. As immature as he was, Bruiser considered his wife to be the reason why Daren was laughing at him. Bruiser maintained this belief rather than take any responsibility for his own criminality. It never occurred to him that Daren's ridicule might be justified.

Knowing her husband as well as she did, Emily felt certain he would become violent once the call with Daren ended.

Daren's final insult, the final twist of the knife, came when he said Emily should be the one to bring the hunting equipment to Daren's plantation in Jackson, Tennessee. Admonishing Bruiser, Daren said, "Because you cannot own a gun, Emily needs to bring them. After all, we don't want you to break the law." When he said this, with a snide laugh, Daren disconnected.

Having been castigated, humiliated and rebuked, utter hell followed this conversation. Infuriated by what she had learned, Emily demanded an explanation about Bruiser's arrests, but he wasn't in a talking mood. All he wanted to do was pummel her, which he proceeded to do.

Chasing her into the basement, he kicked her until she took cover under the pool table. No longer able to reach her with his foot, Bruiser grabbed a pool cue and poked her with it, while she was trapped beneath the table.

Daren's telephone call had been calculated and deliberate. He knew what Bruiser would do to Emily once the call ended. This is why he insisted Bruiser be at home for the call rather than remain at his office for a three-way conference call. Emily may have been the beneficiary of the coveted perk, but she would receive a terrible beating for it, except to her face. Bruiser's humiliation and Emily's beating delighted Daren Magnus. After all, he was the master of malice.

CHAPTER 9

A Heart Over the "I"

1994

The morning following Daren's revelation about Bruiser's criminal past, while nursing her bruises, Emily still couldn't wrap her mind around everything she learned on the conference call. She couldn't believe she had been married to an embezzling Peeping Tom for more than a decade. That it had taken her nearly thirteen years to discover the complete truth about her husband made her ill, but it was also comical.

Coming from the world of fashion and modeling, the way she was viewed by others was extremely important. Her image was everything. It was the reason why she continued to put on a happy face to the outside world, despite the abuse she endured at the hands of her husband. She didn't want anyone to know the truth about their marriage—not even to suspect there was anything wrong with it. She was determined to keep her misfortune hidden from everyone.

She wasn't alone in feeling this way. Nearly all battered women have the same desire.

Emily was determined that nobody would discover the truth about her husband—that his business life was shady, that his nature was that of a sexual deviant or that he treated her like the star of "Punch & Judy Show." Keeping her personal misery to herself was comforting. Not allowing others to discover her plight consoled her but, even in her darkest hours, she never suspected Bruiser had been arrested multiple times for being a Peeping Tom.

That he was a pervert and a sexual deviant was shocking but it was also amusing. She wondered how a bully could also be a voyeur. Such a combination seemed incongruous.

When she thought about the lengths to which she had gone to shelter Bruiser and their reputation as a couple, she suddenly realized that everything she had fought to protect had been a complete waste of time. All that was required to strip away her camouflage, her micro-thin veneer of respectability, was access to a computer where anyone who was interested could run a police report. For $50 or less. For chump change, her marital partner could be exposed, and she couldn't do a thing in the world to prevent it. His deviancy and criminality, which were part of the public record, made a mockery of her desire for respectability.

Daren's call also made her realize something else. Bruiser would never be the man she desired him to be. Even if he was willing to do everything she asked him to do, which would never be the case, he didn't have the character qualities required to be a decent human being. It simply wasn't part of his nature to be an honorable, forthright or honest man and it never had been there.

By beating her and treating her with contempt, Bruiser was simply being himself. It's who he really was. Although finally admitting this to herself nearly killed her, she now accepted that he was never going to change. He wasn't capable of it.

She wondered if he had always been like this? She knew the answer, of course, but she was now willing to admit it to herself. She felt like a fool to have allowed herself to be so badly deceived.

Reflecting, she thought about what Bruiser had been like when they met on her mother's patio thirteen years earlier. Allowing her mind to drift back to 1994, she visualized their first meeting.

Having returned home from a modeling assignment, after parking her car, Emily walked out of the garage onto her mother's patio. This was when she first spotted James Chambers. He was standing right there in front of her. Not expecting to see anyone, Emily was startled. Taking a closer look, she saw a tall, mahogany-tanned Adonis standing before her. He was very athletic, lean and muscular. He didn't have an ounce of extra weight on him. Seeing how handsome he was, she was so shocked that she was actually close to being speechless.

Walking over to her, rather than introducing himself, he asked. "Do you live here?"

"Yes, this is my home," Emily responded, finally finding her voice.

Bruiser was the co-owner of a construction company at the time and also a contractor who did home renovations. He had been working on the townhouse diagonally behind Emily's mother's home. The two places were so close together their garages almost touched.

Unfortunately, Emily's house had just flooded. The water hose to the washing machine had burst the previous night. The following morning Emily and her mother were greeted by three feet of water that had engulfed their entire first floor. Everything was ruined.

Since Bruiser and his partner had been working on the neighbor's house, Emily's mom asked him to drop by and give her an estimate about how much it would cost to make the necessary repairs. This was the reason why Bruiser was standing on the patio. He was assessing the damage to provide a restoration estimate.

Emily recalled thinking that Bruiser must have been a professional athlete. He was that strong, that muscular and that self-confident.

Because she had just returned from her modeling assignment, Emily was dressed to the nines. Plus, she was still wearing her professionally-applied makeup. She looked gorgeous, which Bruiser noticed instantly. Clearly, he was interested.

Being mutually mesmerized, a spark was lit between them. Their attraction was instantaneous, even though Bruiser was not the type of man Emily usually dated.

Instead of the young, muscular, athletic type, Emily generally preferred older men. Her type was a man in his mid-forties to early-fifties. She liked guys that had salt and pepper hair and were no taller than six feet. If possible, she also preferred her dates to be Jewish, but this wasn't a requirement.

Although Bruiser didn't fit any of Emily's preferred categories, there the two of them stood, face to face, on her mother's patio, staring at each other. The chemistry was so powerful it was practically magnetic. Despite the awkwardness of the moment, it was equally exhilarating.

Bruiser finally said, "Hey, let's get some Mexican food. I know a great place."

Still in shock at seeing this bronzed god standing on her mother's patio, all Emily could verbalize was a flimsy, "Yes, okay."

Recovering her composure soon thereafter, Emily began to talk herself out of going to dinner with Bruiser. Her first instinct was that it was a really bad idea, especially since she was pursuing a long-distance relationship with a handsome, wealthy stockbroker from Boca Raton, Florida. This older man, who fit her criteria for a suitable mate to a tee, was smart, personable and dressed fashionably. Best of all, he was always proud to be with Emily and treated her like a princess.

His house was on the intracoastal waterway. He also had a super yacht that was even more spectacular than his home. Going to dinner with him meant that a maid or a valet would pick out her outfit. When they dined, they loved to make a spectacular entrance. Because her boyfriend always docked his yacht at the restaurant, their entrances were spectacular.

When they walked in, with him being uber rich and her being a fashion model, a hush would fall over everyone at the restaurant, patrons and wait staff alike. Everyone would glance at them and wonder if they were celebrities. They weren't, but Emily always felt that they were when she was with him.

Emily loved their lifestyle and hoped their relationship might become permanent. Her boyfriend talked about getting married frequently but that was the problem. All it ever amounted to was talk. The man said that Emily could have any type of wedding she wanted. The sky was the limit, but nothing tangible ever eventuated from his vague promises.

By the time she inadvertently met Bruiser, Emily felt certain her relationship with the stockbroker in Florida was nothing but a dead end street. So, when Bruiser asked Emily to have Mexican food that afternoon, she agreed immediately. He suggested they take Emily's car. When she asked why, he said that his truck wasn't appropriate for a date.

Genuinely enjoying each other's company, they laughed throughout the meal, connecting at a level she never experienced with her boyfriend in Florida.

On the way home later that evening, Bruiser looked at Emily and said. "Damn it, I'm going to marry you!"

Emily laughed at this "ridiculous comment" from the over-confident contractor. Nevertheless, less than a month later, they became engaged. They couldn't get married right away, however. As it turned out, Bruiser was already married. They needed to wait until his divorce became final.

• • •

Although Emily had always wanted a small wedding, what she ended up having wasn't even close to her heart's desire. When she asked her mother for financial help, Emily was informed, "There isn't any money for a wedding. You can get married like the rest of the women in our family, at the courthouse or in our living room."

Despite this setback, which felt more like a rebuke, Emily moved relentlessly forward. Other problems materialized. No rabbi would marry them because Bruiser wasn't Jewish. Undeterred, they tried the Catholic Church, where they were informed that no priest would marry them either. The reason was because Emily was Jewish.

As fate would have it, their first date was on Friday the 13th, so they decided to get married on October 13th, which was immediately after

Bruiser's divorce became final.

More red flags emerged. Bruiser couldn't pay for any of the wedding expenses. Making one concession after another, the wedding Emily had visualized since her childhood completely vanished. Every wedding expense—her dress, her bouquet, the suite at the Ritz Carlton and even Bruiser's boutonniere—were placed on one of her credit cards. Bruiser couldn't pay for anything.

Interestingly, another problem developed concerning Emily's credit cards. When she was introduced to Bruiser's parents, immediately after entering their home for the first time, Bruiser's father asked to take Emily's coat and purse. He told her he would put them on the bed in the guest room. Thinking nothing of it, Emily handed her light-weight jacket and purse to Bruiser's chivalrous father.

While Bruiser's father had her purse, he rifled through it and helped himself to Emily's Visa card, MasterCard and La Elegancia Fashion Boutique card. Not expecting to be robbed, Emily didn't notice the credit cards were missing for quite a while.

When she finally discovered the theft, Bruiser had a serious row with his sticky-fingered father, but the damage had already been done. Although Emily did retrieve her credit cards, she was saddled with the hefty bills Bruiser's father had charged to them. She couldn't go to the police and have Bruiser's parents arrested either, not and risk the imprisonment of her future father-in-law. So, she ended up having to pay the bills herself.

Going through each charge they made, she noticed that both of his parents signed their names with a heart over the "I." Bless their hearts. What a pair, she thought.

Being devout Catholics, although they never attended mass, they self-righteously refused to attend the wedding of a "Jewess." In fact, when Bruiser informed them he intended to marry Emily, Bruiser's mother replied. "You're going to marry a Jew!" His horrified mother added, "How could you do this to us? We don't want a Jew in our family."

When Bruiser told Emily about this, he added that he hated his parents anyway and always had. He didn't care if they attended the wedding or not. He concluded. "It would be better if they did not come, especially after they robbed you."

Genuinely offended by what these cretins had done and said about her, Emily was relieved. She certainly didn't want them at her wedding, so she scratched his parents off of the guest list. She never regretted doing so.

Emily's mother was different. She liked Bruiser. They got along famously, but the woman refused to take time off from work to attend her own daughter's wedding. Obviously, being slighted by her mother about the most important day in in her life hurt Emily deeply. It was a pain that never went away.

Concerning whom to invite, Bruiser could not come up with the name of even one friend who wanted to attend. With no one from her side of the family coming, Emily finally asked a modeling friend to be her maid of honor. She then asked another friend to be Bruiser's best man.

That Bruiser had no friends began to bother Emily. Finally, when he came to her and said he could not afford to purchase an engagement ring, which had long been promised, Emily was so taken aback that she began to balk. Bruiser even had the gall to present her with a credit application from a jewelry store so that she could finance her own ring.

When he did this, Emily got cold feet. There were just too many things going against them. After several sleepless nights, Emily finally decided to call off the wedding. When she informed Bruiser, she expected him to accept her decision gracefully, but he didn't. Instead, he responded by bullying her to the point that she was so afraid of what he might do that she decided to proceed with the wedding.

As a result, on October 13, 1994, Bruiser and Emily were married at the Davidson County courthouse with two acquaintances for their witnesses. For this less-than-joyous occasion, in addition to all of her other expenses, Emily was required to buy her own gown and bouquet. She even paid for Bruiser's suit and tie to go along with the boutonniere she had already purchased.

There were no wedding invitations, just announcements. There was no photographer for the event, no makeup artist, no hairstylist, no cake, no reception and no limousine. After the perfunctory three-minute civil service, Bruiser and Emily went to an Italian restaurant for dinner before heading to the Hilton. Needless to say, she paid for their dinner and also their room.

For Emily, it was barely a wedding, but it was a legally binding contract between the two of them. Concerning their union as a couple, Bruiser told Emily many times afterwards. "This marriage isn't about you; it's about me." At other times, he would add. "What's yours is mine and what's mine is mine."

At first, she thought he was just being playful but, based on numerous painful situations that followed, she knew he meant exactly what he said. This self-serving saying, "What's yours is mine and what's mine is mine," became his mantra during their entire marriage.

CHAPTER 10

A Solid Grip on Her Rear

2003

True to his word, Bruiser's relationship with Emily was all about him. Everything was always about him and never about her. Emily was simply an appendage. She was there to help him become whatever he envisioned himself to be and, like the spoiled four-year-old that he was, whenever he didn't get his way in exactly the way he wanted it, he threw a violent temper tantrum.

If Emily crossed him in any way, if things didn't proceed precisely the way he desired, or if he didn't like the outcome of an event for any reason, he would lash out at her verbally and physically. He made their marriage a veritable nightmare.

Doing her best to keep the peace, Emily learned to walk on eggshells whenever Bruiser's mood turned dark or he had too much to drink. Each day was like this. There was never a break in the action, never a time when Emily could let down her guard and simply be herself.

Even though Emily was forced to finance their wedding, it wasn't because Bruiser was penniless. He had an excellent job following his short stint as a contractor. He made good money working for the Southern Company, but all of this ended abruptly one day, without a word of warning.

One afternoon Bruiser came home quite early. With a crestfallen look on his face, he informed Emily he had lost his job. Adding insult to injury, he told her he had actually been escorted out of his office by two security guards. Once he reached the outside door, they informed him that he would never be allowed to set foot in the building again, not even to retrieve his personal belongings. They would be delivered to him via UPS.

The reason he was fired was because the consulting company that had the contract with the Southern Company ran a background check on him. When they did, they discovered he had been arrested for fishing without a license. At least, this is what he told Emily. At the time, she had no clue about how long his rap sheet really was. Bruiser certainly didn't inform her about it either. It would be years before she actually discovered the complete, unvarnished truth, thanks to the conference call with Daren Magnus.

Having been arrested, however, disqualified Bruiser from working for the company's high security BAT team. BAT was an acronym for "Business Application Testing Group."

Bruiser loved his position at the Southern Company. His job was to test security applications for the company's nuclear energy facilities. It was a lucrative and prestigious position—one that Bruiser relished holding.

Since he had already been employed by his company for nearly seven years, he was surprised they would go to the trouble of performing a background check, but they did. That someone like Bruiser, who had so many arrests could have ever been employed for so long must have surprised the company but, when they discovered their error, they dealt with their felonious employee swiftly.

Surprised that such a minor offense would disqualify her husband, Emily was very supportive of Bruiser, telling him how unfairly he had been treated. Her support, however, wasn't nearly enough to pacify her deeply-wounded husband. The humiliation of being escorted out of the building by security guards infuriated and embittered him.

The afternoon of his dismissal, to calm himself, Bruiser poured himself three fingers of Scotch. Sipping it in solitude, he became increasingly sullen and morose, as a quiet storm began to build within him.

Recognizing the signs of what was about to happen, Emily did not challenge him about drinking too much. Fearful of setting him off, she refrained from saying a disparaging word about anything. Instead, she began to think of ways she could extricate herself from his presence until he calmed down and sobered up. Having been the recipient of his angry aggression in the past, she had no desire to remain in harm's way, but she couldn't think of a valid reason to extricate herself. Although she wanted to, she couldn't just leave. Resigned to her fate, she did her best to avoid initiating a conflict. She hoped that by being calm and peaceful she could weather the storm, but her strategy of avoidance proved to be ineffective.

Finally, influenced by Scotch, he snapped. Railing at her, the Southern Company and the unfairness of life in general, Bruiser lost his temper. He believed they were going to lose their house. Even worse, he felt certain he would lose his motorcycle—his pride and joy. In his bitterness, he also believed his co-workers were thrilled to witness his humiliation. He was sure they were mocking him, when he was being escorted out of the building by uniformed guards. He hated them for this.

This unwarranted humiliation was such an affront to his massive, fragile ego that it finally drove him over the edge to violence—that plus consuming a heavy dose of Scotch. Becoming increasingly volatile, he screamed at Emily that she meant nothing to him. She was just a burden.

Escalating his verbal abuse, he said she did nothing and was worth nothing. In his cruelty, he scorned her, telling her that even her own mother preferred him over her, but that wasn't enough. He couldn't even be satisfied to leave it at that. Instead, becoming physical, he slammed Emily against the hallway wall. Twisting her face to be within an inch of his own, he screamed at her to "get out of his house. Do something worthwhile," he demanded.

Bruiser was so close to her that his Scotch-laden spit sprayed her. Before he relinquished his tight grip on her, his spittle was literally dripping from her chin.

Emily was terrified. Being emotional by nature, she wanted to cry but she didn't. She knew better than to shed a tear. Bruiser wouldn't stand for that. If she allowed herself to cry, it would make her situation much worse and she knew it. With no alternative, she stood there and took his verbal and physical abuse, hoping it would run its course and end.

This is what Bruiser was really like. This was the man Emily chose to marry, going deep into debt to do so. Consistently cruel and harsh, he was never comforting or consoling. Only weak men behaved that way, according to her abusive husband. He would never apologize for his behavior either. Again, only weak men apologized, and Bruiser certainly was not a weak man, at least not in his own eyes.

To survive emotionally, when Bruiser's behavior turned violent, Emily taught herself to go someplace else in her mind. She was forced to exit his presence emotionally with increasing frequency. This was necessary because her husband's violent episodes were escalating.

That evening, having lost interest in punishing Emily for his unfair treatment at the Southern Company, Bruiser finally released her with a sudden jerk. Gasping for breath, she quickly headed to the foyer and prepared to leave the house, just in case he decided to attack her again. With his glass nearing empty, however, Bruiser was much more interested in refilling it than he was in pursuing his confrontation with his wife.

• • •

Having lost his contract to work with the Southern Company, Bruiser pushed very hard to become a full-time employee at Leipers Fork Harley, where he had been working part-time for quite a while. To make this happen, he lied, informing them he had graduated from Texas A&M. Maintaining that he was a computer expert with a degree from A&M, Daren's company hired him, giving him a contract that paid him $10,000 per month.

In his efforts to make a good impression at Leipers Fork Harley, Bruiser brought Emily to the facility to meet everybody. Because his wife was a strikingly beautiful model, Bruiser wanted everybody to recognize what a man of stature he was.

One of the partners at the Harley dealership was a man named Jud Norbert. When Bruiser introduced Emily to Jud, she disliked this man instantly. He was crude, arrogant, vulgar and boastful. Worse, he treated those who worked for him like servants. Being one of Daren's financial advisors, Jud had somehow manipulated Daren into making him a part owner of the dealership.

That Jud was able to accomplish this impressed Bruiser. He thought that if he could get close enough to Daren, precisely like Jud had done, Daren might make him wealthy too. Because being rich was Bruiser's goal in life, getting close to Daren became Bruiser's primary vocational objective. Because Daren was rarely present at Leipers Fork Harley back in 2003, however, this proved to be very difficult.

At the dealership, the employees actually considered Daren Magnus to be a ghost. He was talked about constantly, but he was rarely present. Despite being the principal owner of the dealership, he didn't even have his own office.

Even Emily was growing curious about who Daren was—the man whose name only had one 'R' and not two. To her, it didn't seem like the dealership had any real leadership. For all of Jud's efforts to look like he was the boss—the big man on campus—it was quite clear he wasn't.

One of the "motor-hoes," the nickname Harley women were given, had attended high school with Daren. All she would say about him was that he "was a partier." Everybody was proud of this. Apparently, this man-child, Daren Magnus, could still party like a teenager, even though he was middle-aged.

One time, Jud Norbert proudly informed Emily that he and Daren were able to "hose down cocaine" like it was Pez candy. Although Jud thought this would impress Emily, it had the exact opposite effect. She was appalled, especially coming from a Neanderthal like Jud.

Emily loathed Jud. He was a fat, repulsive, scraggly man with an unkempt goatee. He thought this made him look cool, but it actually made him look ridiculous. As mercurial as his personality was, Emily suspected he might be bipolar. Nevertheless, he seemed to be the happiest man at the dealership, while also being the most selfish.

The angriest man at Leipers Fork was Bruiser. With a leadership team like this, Emily wondered what Daren would be like. Everyone knew he was wealthy, but what else? Emily wondered about this a great deal.

Leipers Fork's grand opening was scheduled for September 1, 2003. As the date approached, Bruiser, who was still just a part-time employee at the dealership, wanted Emily to be present for the event. Knowing she would make him look good, he wanted her to meet everyone. Although he wasn't proud of her, he did realize her presence would enhance his stature at the dealership. Sadly, this was the closest thing of paying Emily a compliment that a narcissist like Bruiser was capable of doing.

Although Jud may have been part owner of Leipers Fork, he was nothing more than a Daren Magnus wannabe. Once, when Jud spotted Emily at the dealership, knowing it was her birthday, as well as the grand opening at Leipers Fork, he said. "I'm going to give you a big hug, girl."

With that, he grabbed Emily's derriere with both hands and forcefully pressed his body against hers, grinding his crotch into hers. Startled, Emily was livid. Because his hug was more like sexual groping than a fraternal hug, she tried to pull herself away from him as vigorously as she could, but she couldn't extricate herself from his firm grip. He was much too strong.

Bruiser witnessed the entire event. Although he walked over to Jud, he didn't confront the man. In fact, he didn't say a word about Jud dry-humping his wife, which was precisely what Jud was doing. Bruiser didn't protest or protect Emily in any way. Instead, he just watched his wife be humiliated. Little did she know it at the time but this was an experience that would be replicated numerous times by Jud, much to her chagrin.

With the situation remaining tense, Jud suddenly turned his head. When he did, he released Emily instantly, stepped away from her and raced up the staircase two steps at a time. Because of his obesity, this required significant effort. He did this because Daren Magnus had been standing at the top of the railing, watching the entire event.

As surprising as it might seem, it was Daren who actually came to Emily's rescue. This is how she finally met the mysterious principal owner of Leipers Fork Harley. The "ghost man" finally materialized. Although this was the first and probably last time Emily would be happy to see Daren Magnus, she was delighted he was there.

He was taller than she had imagined. Perhaps he was about 6'1'. He was definitely in good shape too. He was a runner who jogged constantly. He had blonde hair, piercing blue eyes and, because he jogged and rode a motorcycle, he was well tanned. Emily noticed immediately that Daren didn't have any tattoos. This was rare in the Harley world. He was not wearing any biker clothing either.

As nice looking as Daren was, his face wasn't a happy one. To Emily, there seemed to be an aura of evil about him, a sense of danger and malice that shrouded his entire countenance. He was quite intimidating, making her feel very uncomfortable. She felt this way even though Daren had just saved her from Jud's rapacious birthday hug.

Because Daren did not introduce himself, Jud did it, despite being out of breath from climbing the stairs.

Jud wheezed. "Emily, this is Daren."

Emily replied. "Ah, the man who needs no introduction."

Having begun to walk downstairs by this time, being accompanied by his sycophantic partner, Daren finally met Emily. He never offered his hand to her though. Once he reached the bottom of the staircase, he just stood there for a long moment appraising her. Then, he walked off without saying a word.

A moment later, Jud and Bruiser followed him into an office where they shut the door, leaving Emily to stand there alone, feeling terribly awkward.

About thirty minutes later, the three men reappeared. Walking up to Emily, Daren said, "I hear it's your birthday."

Smiling, Emily replied. "Yes, it is."

Leading the way, Daren said. "Then, come with me. There's cake."

Hearing this, Emily was surprised but delighted. There was a birthday cake for her. She believed this briefly but this was before she saw the cake. When she did, she was instantly brought back to reality. Most of the cake had already been eaten. It had been purchased for the grand opening of the dealership.

All that remained of the sheet cake was the "gr" and "ope," which originally stood for, "Grand Opening." Somehow that the word "Grope" was what remained seemed oddly appropriate. Perhaps it was a cosmic foreshadowing of what had just happened and what was to come.

Daren cut Emily a piece of cake and handed it to her. Then, being magnanimous, he also handed her a plastic fork, saying, "Enjoy."

Although the cake was dry, stale and tasteless, she ate it anyway, knowing that doing so might be important for her husband. Once she was finished, Daren gave her a tour of each area of the dealership. She thought he behaved very nicely. His conduct even bordered on being gracious, but Emily didn't accept anything about him as being genuine. Instead, her instincts screamed at her, warning her that this man could not be trusted. There was something about him that didn't seem right and she knew it.

Nevertheless, from their first meeting forward, Emily definitely got the impression that Daren liked her, not in a normal way or even in a romantic way but in an unwholesome, lascivious way. It made her feel uncomfortable—like she needed to take a shower. Despite this, unlike her husband, Daren had come to her rescue. Although he had been chivalrous in getting Jud to stop dry-humping her, Emily's spirit was troubled. She knew to never let down her guard when she was in the presence of Daren Magnus.

CHAPTER 11

The Rarely Traveled Road

2007

In 2007, after an investigation that had begun several years earlier in Palm Beach County, Florida, financier Jeffrey Epstein was arrested for soliciting sex from an underage woman. This was not an isolated incident for Epstein but a well-established pattern of behavior. He was heavily involved in sex trafficking. The subsequent inquiry into his deviant activities was extensive. Because many powerful people, including former-President Bill Clinton and the Duke of York, Prince Andrew, had allegedly accompanied Epstein to Orgy Island on Epstein's private jet, dubbed the Lolita Express, news of Epstein's legal situation became headline news throughout the United States and worldwide.

In the Virgin Islands, especially on Saint Thomas, where much of his trafficking and sexual escapades occurred, news of Epstein's arrest sent shockwaves throughout the corrupt island. The impact of Epstein's situation was profound at Estate Viol. Fearing discovery about his own behavior, Daren Magnus and the other pedophile whales became concerned that the investigation into Epstein's activities might eventually be connected to what they were doing.

Because the risk of discovery was so great, Daren Magnus moved swiftly. Immediately after learning the news, Daren put Estate Viol on the market. He shut down Fisherman's North Drop restaurant and abandoned his ongoing operation to defraud the IRS through his EDC.

With the fall of Epstein, Daren didn't want to be around when the FBI started probing into the affairs of people like him—whales who had a penchant for raping underage girls. Daren shut his operation in Saint Thomas down fast, liquidating everything. Just a few months later, it was as if he had never been on the island. This was precisely the goal he intended to achieve.

The decision to leave Saint Thomas impacted the lives of Bruiser and Emily Chambers in a significant way. For her, it was a relief. As sick of travel as she had become, coupled with being required to turn a blind eye to the high turnover in hostesses at the restaurant, Emily looked forward to staying at home in their lovely home at Squash, where she would soon become the secretary of the homeowner's association.

She did so well at this task that the homeowner's association honored her at one of their well-attended meetings. During the meeting, when the President of the Squash Homeowner's Association extolled her virtues, Emily received a standing ovation from everyone present, that is everyone except for her husband. He refused to leave his seat.

Bruiser was bitterly resentful that Emily was receiving accolades, especially since their marriage was supposed to be "all about him" and never about her. Offended by her notoriety, he remained seated when everyone else stood. He refused to even clap his hands when others honored Emily with thunderous applause.

Seeing Bruiser's sullen response, which all of their neighbors witnessed, Emily's heart sank. Everybody in attendance recognized her value, why couldn't her husband? His militant, bitter refusal to honor her was so deflating that she wanted to cry but this certainly wasn't an option, not at her own victory celebration. On the inside, however, in the depth of her heart, Bruiser had succeeded in accomplishing his goal. He had robbed her of experiencing even a brief moment of joy.

Because of Bruiser's refusal to stand and cheer, the couple's neighbors recognized that trouble must be brewing at the Chambers's house. Bruiser's childish response made this obvious. What should have been a victory for Emily became the exact opposite. She knew everybody in the neighborhood would be talking about them, which was the last thing she wanted. More than anything, she had gone to extraordinary lengths to keep their marital dysfunction private. Now, thanks to Bruiser's peevishness, even this was gone. Knowing that her personal angst would now become the talk of the neighborhood, Emily's heart sank.

• • •

Exactly one week before her birthday that year, Emily planned to spend the day running errands. Making a decision at the last moment to take her Mercedes SUV instead of her Volkswagen convertible, she headed out. Taking the scenic route, she pulled out of her driveway and turned down a rarely traveled road. Part of it had not even been paved. It was just an old country road, but it was also very beautiful.

As she continued, reaching the paved road soon thereafter, she saw a landscaping truck pulling a long trailer. Because it was loaded with lawn equipment, it was moving slowly. On the far side of the truck, Emily noticed a fast-moving Lexus convertible. Because there was a curve in the two-lane road, Emily lost sight of the Lexus, but she could still see the landscaping truck coming toward her in the opposite lane.

The next thing she saw was the Lexus. It had crossed the double yellow line and was headed straight for her at a high rate of speed. What happened next seemed like a blur that happened in slow-motion. The Lexus struck her Mercedes SUV so violently that part of the Lexus actually went underneath Emily's SUV. The force of the impact was so severe that her SUV spun around in a series of circles, nearly rolling over.

The SUV's airbag deployed, pinning Emily while the vehicle continued to lurch dangerously from side to side. At this precise moment, she lost consciousness.

The next thing she remembered was feeling tremendous pain. She hurt all over. Hearing a commotion coming from numerous directions, she realized that the Mexican landscapers were desperately trying to open her car door, but they were having difficulty doing so. In her dazed state, she couldn't understand why they wanted to open her door. And why were all of these men standing around her car? And what were they saying? She couldn't understand a word. And why did her right foot hurt so badly?

Such were the disjointed thoughts of a woman who had just sustained a concussion.

The accident bent the frame to her Mercedes so badly that the driver's side door simply would not open. That it wouldn't was very confusing to her. While they continued tugging and pulling, she started to become more lucid.

As she did, she felt a sharp, stinging pain in her neck. It was in the same spot that had been injured the night Bruiser threw her violently into the marble wet bar months earlier. The pain felt like the sting of a wasp.

Reaching for her purse, which was on the passenger side floor, she heard several of the landscaper's yell, "she's moving;" "she's conscious;" and "she's alive." Hearing this seemed odd. She couldn't imagine who they were talking about, but at least they were speaking in English.

Finally reaching her purse, which was difficult with the airbag having been deployed, she grabbed her cellphone and called 911. Telling the operator what had happened as best she could, despite her words being somewhat disjointed, the woman told her to stay in her vehicle. The operator was concerned Emily might have sustained a life-threatening injury from the crash.

By this time, the landscapers had used a crowbar to successfully pry open the driver's side door. While the 911 operator remained on the phone, Emily heard the siren of a Rutherford County Sheriff's vehicle approaching. Once her door was open, one of the Mexicans used a knife to deflate the airbag. Then, he reached around Emily and released her seatbelt, allowing her to get out of her mangled Mercedes, despite being admonished to stay put. A fire truck arrived moments later.

Also arriving at about the same time, the sheriff's deputy approached Emily while she was leaning against her car. He asked if she needed an ambulance.

Still groggy, Emily answered. "No, I don't think so."

As injured as she was, she probably should have said yes, but she didn't. The deputy was young and about Bruiser's size, but there was a stark difference between the two men. The sheriff's deputy was genuinely kind and very attentive to Emily's needs, which Bruiser would never condescend to do.

After making certain Emily was okay, the deputy attended to the needs of driver of the Lexus convertible. Thankfully, they were minimal. It was obvious the other driver was inebriated. She had been speeding because she was late to pick up her kids from school.

The woman seemed familiar to Emily, but she wasn't certain from where. Ironically, Emily later discovered the woman had purchased a Harley from Leipers Fork. Predictably, the woman had also totaled her motorcycle. Emily wondered if she had been drinking when she wrecked her motorcycle too, but she never asked.

As shaken as she was, Emily needed to speak to her husband, but her initial call went to his voicemail. Trying again, this time it didn't even ring. It went straight to his voicemail. She realized Bruiser was screening her calls and wouldn't permit himself to be bothered, not by her.

A few minutes later, once the deputy finished attending to the other driver, he came back to Emily and asked if he could call anyone for her. He also wanted to know if she needed a ride home.

Responding, Emily said. "No thank you, but would you please try to call my husband?"

"Certainly," the young deputy replied. When he called, Bruiser answered immediately. The sheriff's deputy told Bruiser his wife had just been in a very serious car accident.

While the officer was speaking, Emily looked at the young man's face. When she did, she noticed a significance alteration in his countenance. She would never forget his change of expression.

Responding to a question Bruiser asked, the officer said. "No, the car is totaled." Then, the young man asked. "Don't you want to know about your wife?"

Obviously, Bruiser didn't care as much about Emily's safety as he did the fate of their beautiful Mercedes SUV, but this didn't surprise Emily. How could it? She felt certain her husband never considered the seriousness of her condition.

When the call ended, the deputy looked at Emily and said cheerfully. "Hey, how about I drive you home?"

By the officer's response, Emily knew for certain her husband had not asked about her condition. Bruiser's only concern was about the status of the car.

Eventually, Bruiser did arrive at the scene. By the time he did, the flatbed wrecker had finished placing Emily's car on it to be towed away. As she was sitting in the front seat of the officer's cruiser, Bruiser practically bolted out of his car to look at the Mercedes. Predictably, he was mad. Seeing the look of fury on Bruiser's face, Emily just shook her head. It seemed like her husband spent most of his life being mad at something or someone, especially her, but she was past fretting about his mood.

Their marriage, which had been on life support for quite some time, was nearing its end. She could feel it in her bones, at least the bones that didn't hurt from the accident.

Seeing how indifferent Bruiser was to his injured wife, including how badly she had been shaken, the young deputy came over to Emily one last time. Imploringly, he asked. "Are you sure you don't want me to take you home?"

"No, but thank you so much," Emily replied, grateful for the caring of a complete stranger.

Bruiser finally came over to the deputy's car to speak to Emily. With no compassion in his voice whatsoever, he snapped. "Can't you walk?"

"Yes," she replied, "but it hurts like hell when I do."

Taking a quick look at her neck and right ankle, Bruiser said. "I guess you should go to the hospital." With that, he walked over to his car to drive her to the ER. Emily, who was unable to keep pace with him, hobbled behind painfully. Bruiser never offered to help—not even to open the door for her.

While driving to the Rutherford County ER, he yelled at her for wrecking the Mercedes. Defending herself as best she could, Emily repeatedly told him she had been hit by a drunk driver, explaining that the woman had crossed the double yellow line.

Finally standing up for herself, she protested adamantly. "The accident was not my fault."

Not once during their drive to the hospital did he ask about how she was doing. What bothered him the most, other than the fact she had totaled their Mercedes, was her accident had interrupted a speed test for his new Harley. That she had nearly died from a head on collision was a real inconvenience to him. She had ruined his day and he let her know how displeased he was about it.

CHAPTER 12

He Would Eventually Go to Jail

SEPTEMBER-OCTOBER 2007

Bruiser continued to blame Emily for the accident, repeatedly pointing a condemning finger at her. He did this until something unexpected happened. Daren called Emily to check up on how she was doing. Once this happened, once Daren absolved Emily of any negligence by reaching out to her, so did Bruiser. All was forgiven. Since it was never Emily's wrongdoing in the first place, Bruiser's persistent fault-finding had been insulting and infuriating. This made her grateful for Daren's intervention. Although unexpected, this was the second time Daren had come to her rescue.

Being validated and absolved by Daren put an end to Bruiser's verbal assault. Because he could not pass the background check to own either the Harley dealership in Cocke County or Jackson, Emily's importance to Daren's operation heightened considerably. Predictably, this continued to be a thorn in Bruiser's side. After all, their marriage was all about him and never about her. Nevertheless, the situation imposed upon them by the Harley-Davidson Corporation was beyond Bruiser's control. Daren couldn't control it either. The determining factor was Harley's corporate policy.

To be the principal owner, even in name only, Emily was required to be on site. This meant the Chambers would need to sell their beautiful home at Squash and move to Jackson. This was something Emily did not want to do and she let her feelings be known. Having come to believe Daren was doing nothing but playing her, she didn't want to leave Rutherford County.

Predictably, the couple argued about this repeatedly. Something had to give and it finally did. Daren discovered Harley's corporate policy wouldn't allow anyone to be married to a spouse who couldn't pass the background check either. The reason for this was based on the company's inheritance policy. Harley Davidson wouldn't allow someone like Bruiser to become the owner, even if something tragic were to happen to his wife. Although this seemed ridiculous to Emily when she first learned about it, she probably should have welcomed the news. It created a great insurance policy for her, ensuring her survival.

Because of this impediment to Daren's plans, he had to improvise further. Doing so, he called Emily and told her matter-of-factly that she needed to divorce Bruiser. "There's no way around it," he said, doing his best to persuade her.

Daren said it precisely this way. He was that matter-of-fact about it, but that's not all. While their divorce was pending, Daren told Emily that Bruiser should move to Jackson and find a suitable home for them. While there, he would be able to set up the Jackson Harley dealership.

Emily's job was to hire movers, organize the packing of their home at Squash and move to Jackson. While still in Rutherford County, she needed to work on obtaining a divorce.

When Emily heard Daren's latest proposal, at first she couldn't believe he was being serious, but he was. He was dead serious. Rather than go along with his scheme to circumvent Harley's corporate policy like her husband wanted her to do, she was offended. That her marriage and her entire life would have to be disassembled and discarded, just to facilitate Daren's desire to make more money, was appalling, infuriating and unacceptable to Emily.

When Bruiser walked in the front door, she told her husband precisely how she felt the minute he entered. That he was willing to go along with this hairbrained scheme of Daren's offended her and she told him so in no uncertain terms.

By confronting Bruiser, not withholding any punches, she initiated a tremendous fight, but she didn't care. Daren had definitely crossed a red line with her. Getting a divorce just so they could conform with Harley's corporate inheritance policy was unacceptable. She felt this way even though she wasn't necessarily against ending her nightmare relationship with Bruiser. What bothered her the most was she did not want to move from the home she loved—not on a whim of Daren's.

She told Bruiser that no human being had ever had as negative an impact on a marriage as Daren had had on theirs. According to Emily, even though her husband was a bully and always had been, he was nothing more than a sniveling coward where Daren Magnus was concerned. Point blank, Emily asked her husband why he was unable and unwilling to stand up for himself or for their marriage?

That he couldn't or wouldn't, refusing to answer her, was contemptible. Challenging his manhood, she definitely put herself in harm's way, but she wanted to let Bruiser know exactly how she felt about everything.

Daren hated marriage. Emily was certain of it. He resented vows and mocked those who chose to be loyal and faithful to each other. After all the damage Daren had caused on Saint Thomas, Emily told Bruiser that she would never trust Daren. Nevertheless, she wisely refrained from mentioning the primary reason for her distrust. Even at the height of her anger toward her husband, Emily maintained their no-talk rule about what happened to the missing hostesses.

Finally allowing her pent-up frustration to vent, which she should have done years earlier, she told Bruiser she didn't believe Daren would keep his promise. She said they would "never own a Harley dealership."

Bruiser was equally certain they would and told Emily so, doing his best to counter each of her arguments. Because they needed her to pull off Daren's sleight of hand with Harley Davidson, Bruiser couldn't simply beat her into submission. Although this had always been his default position, he realized it wouldn't work this time.

Daren continued to work on Emily. To get her onboard with this scheme, he told her she would become the general manager of the Jackson dealership and have her own independent salary. That he was willing to do that surprised her. Knowing she needed to establish financial independence from Bruiser, this appealed to her a great deal. After everything she had been through, a job with a good salary sounded wonderful. With her own paycheck, she could achieve financial freedom and, if she played her cards right, it would also provide her with a way out of her disastrous situation.

Therefore, she finally acquiesced. The week after her birthday, about ten days after being involved un a near fatal accident, Bruiser packed up his clothes and moved to Jackson, Tennessee. With everything she had been through, she wasn't unhappy to see him walk out the door.

This time, things would be different, or at least she talked herself into believing they would be. Because they needed her, she could no longer be considered an expendable pawn. She had status and worth—a chip in the game. She loved this, even though she feared it was just another devious manipulation by Daren. The cost to Emily was her home and the façade of her marriage to Bruiser, but the reward might be greater. It was a risk she was willing to take.

• • •

In October, nearly a month after Bruiser moved out, Emily became extremely ill with pneumonia. She called her husband and asked him to please come home to help her. Instead of coming, he cursed her for calling and refused to return any of her subsequent calls.

This hardened Emily's heart further. Apparently, caring for her in sickness and health wasn't an applicable vow—not where she was concerned. That Bruiser simply didn't care enough about whether she lived or died to even return her calls was the final blow to their dysfunctional relationship.

Emily had not been abusive, but Bruiser had been repeatedly. Emily had not had affairs and flings, while her husband had participated in numerous escapades. Because he had followed his billionaire mentor around like a whipped dog, Emily lost all respect for the man she married. Although she had stuck by him through each of his melanoma treatments, included three major surgeries, and had been firmly committed to her marital vows, there had never been any reciprocity. Now that she was very sick and needed his help, he refused to return home or even check up on her.

Bruiser had told Emily he was staying at a hotel across the street from the Jackson dealership. She discovered this was a lie. He had actually moved into an apartment with the assistant general manager, a man named Kenneth. Almost immediately, Bruiser became involved with Kenneth's live-in girlfriend, Gidget.

Unbeknownst to Emily, within a short period of time, Gidget dumped Kenneth and became Bruiser's fiancée. This happened while he still married to her. Not surprisingly, since he done the exact same thing with her more than a decade earlier, Bruiser neglected to mention that he was still married. Although he went to high school with Kenneth, Bruiser had no qualms about replacing his old friend in Gidget's bed.

"Gidget Midget" is what everybody called her at the Harley dealership because she was diminutive. Barely five feet tall, she was cute, personable and very sexy. She was also covered with tattoos. This made her a perfect fit for a Harley job. She quickly became the sales manager at the fledgling dealership in Jackson.

During one of the rare times Bruiser spoke to Emily on the phone, he informed her that Gidget and Kenneth were having relationship problems. Hearing this, Emily immediately suspected Bruiser was the reason for Kenneth and Gidget's problems, but she kept her suspicions to herself. Having become secretly engaged, the two lovers quickly got rid of Kenneth.

Unbeknownst to Emily, Bruiser told everyone in Jackson that he was already divorced. This was a lie, of course, Bruiser's specialty. They hadn't even filed the paperwork. When Emily learned what he had been telling others, she realized the end was even closer than she expected.

Bruiser wanted to get rid of her quickly and move on. Two weeks later, he appeared at Squash unexpectedly. He arrived pulling a huge Harley trailer behind his car. In her heart, Emily knew this was the end, but she dreaded the impending conflict it would create.

Sure enough, Bruiser stormed into the house. Without even greeting her, he announced. "We have to get you a car."

Emily replied, "Okay, I want another Mercedes. It saved my life."

Responding, Bruiser announced, "Daren likes BMWs so we're going to look at them."

Emily reiterated that she wanted the exact same car that she had, a Mercedes SUV.

Mockingly, Bruiser rebuffed her. "Too fucking bad, Emily. Daren likes BMWs."

"Well, I am not Daren," Emily protested. "I don't want a BMW. I want another Mercedes SUV." Apparently, the Volkswagen Convertible she already had in the garage wasn't enough for her.

Now furious because of her reluctance, Bruiser responded. "I don't give a fuck what you want. You are going to drive a BMW and it's going to be in your name."

The reason for putting the car in her name was to burden Emily with overwhelming debt. This was a necessary component of the scheme Daren and Bruiser had hatched. If they could accomplish this, they believed they would have better control over her. It would help keep her in line. Part of Daren's overall scheme, which never included Emily having her own paycheck, was to force her into bankruptcy.

Changing the subject, Bruiser announced there was a four-bedroom condo at her mother's subdivision for sale. He said, "We should buy it too."

"But I want to stay at Squash," she pleaded.

"Too fucking bad," he snapped. Even though they were about to be divorced, Bruiser added. "This marriage is about me, not about you."

What she desired didn't matter. It never did. It was never even taken into consideration. Because Emily's name was not on the loan for their Squash home, Bruiser was able to sell it right out from under her without her consent. Unbeknownst to her at the time, Bruiser had already engaged a real estate agent. As a result, their condo at Squash went under contract immediately, without them even negotiating a price. Bruiser wanted out of the marriage fast. This meant Emily would have absolutely no say in the matter.

On the third day after Bruiser arrived home, he ordered Emily to go to her computer and write up their divorce papers.

Emily flatly refused. "We need attorneys, Bruiser," she insisted. "We need to do this properly."

Bruiser replied. "No, we don't! We can do it online. It's cheaper that way."

"I don't care if it is cheaper. I'm not going to do it like this."

Snarling profanities, Bruiser stormed off. Emily was glad to see him go. It provided her with a moment to regroup. She understood that what was about to happen would be important for her future. It might even determine the rest of her life.

When Bruiser reappeared a few minutes later, Emily was terrified by what she saw. In one hand he held a glass of Scotch and in the other hand he held a gun. Knowing how deadly the combination of the two could be, Emily literally shook with fear and trepidation.

Looking at her with malice, knowing he had the upper hand, Bruiser ordered. "You are going online right now to file for divorce."

Without spilling a drop of his precious Scotch, Bruiser shoved her into her office with the point of the gun. He kept prodding her until she was seated behind her computer.

"Type," he ordered.

"No," Emily replied, being more courageous than she had ever been. She felt like she had no choice but to hold her ground.

Undeterred by her refusal, Bruiser slammed the glass down on the desk. Then he lifted the gun and shoved it menacingly into the back of the chair where Emily was sitting, pointing it straight at her.

"You had better start typing," he hissed.

Emily wasn't certain whether or not Bruiser would actually kill her, but her mind flashed back to the underage girls who had gone missing on Saint Thomas. Probably none of them believed they would die either, but they were never heard from again. Wanting to live to fight another day, Emily began to search the Internet for a website where they could obtain the paperwork for an online, uncontested divorce.

Bruiser insisted she type in a lifetime monthly alimony payment. Figuring out what that would be was a chore. Thanks to Daren's mandate, Emily would require a huge car payment for the BMW, as well as a monthly condo payment. With several other payments that Emily would also be required to make, they finally arrived at a figure of $10,000 per month. In addition to this, Bruiser agreed to pay for all of the taxes.

Because the alimony would be for life, this "quickie divorce" was not turning out to be as favorable to Bruiser as he had anticipated. Predictably, this made him angry. Nevertheless, the divorce Emily typed out was exactly what he specified it to be. When he looked at the divorce document he had dictated, with gun and drink in hand, he still wasn't happy—not with a $10,000 monthly payment for life.

Predictably, they bickered back and forth for hours. At midnight, with Bruiser having had quite a bit to drink, Emily became weary of arguing and went to bed. A short while later, Bruiser stormed into the master bedroom and said, "Congratulations, I will sign this divorce and pay you, just like it says I will."

This should have made Emily happy but she was no fool. She was well aware that a divorce drawn up on the Internet with a gun being held to her back would be inadmissible in a court of law. What it was was a criminal act, but its terms were fair.

When she challenged Bruiser about each legitimate expense, like the loan he had taken from Emily's mother several years earlier, Bruiser manned up and agreed to pay the monthly repayment as part of his alimony. By the time they were finished, knowing she did not want to spend the rest of her life with this adulterous bully, she was content to agree to Bruiser's coerced divorce.

In her naiveté, Emily actually thought her nightmare marriage to Bruiser was over, but this was nothing more than wishful thinking. The marriage might have been over, but the nightmare of her divorce had just begun. Despite his repeated promises to do otherwise, Bruiser never had any intention of paying Emily anything, and he would eventually go to jail to prove that he didn't.

THE THREE COMMAS CLUB

CHAPTER 13

Her Year from Hell

FALL 2007 THROUGH 2008

Bruiser, fool that he was, thought he could dictate the terms of his divorce settlement with a gun in one hand and a glass of Johnny Walker Black in the other. That he assumed this would be sufficient was a testimony to his inflated ego and his narcissistic penchant to defer to no authority other than himself. He bowed his knee to nobody other than Daren Magnus and, for better or worse, this would never change.

Satisfied he had made a binding agreement with Emily, he put his gun away, drained his glass of Scotch, packed his personal belongings and headed back to Jackson in the middle of the night. He wanted to be with Gidget, the "tattooed midget."

Gidget, believing she had made a better choice with Bruiser than with her financially strapped fiancée, had discarded Kenneth with a contemptuous sneer. Changing men as easily as she changed sheets, she was thrilled with her good fortune. Believing Bruiser was a better choice, she wanted Emily's life instead of hers.

Beginning his relationship with Gidget based a lie, Bruiser had told her as well as everyone else that his divorce from Emily had already been finalized weeks before. Emily was unaware of any of this, but she definitely had her suspicions about Bruiser's relationship with Gidget. By that point, however, the only thing that bothered her about her marriage coming to an end was how quickly she had been replaced. No woman is ever content with an adulterous termination to her marriage.

After having been absent for a month, once Emily filed for a legitimate divorce, Bruiser was discontent that things had not already been wrapped up. Instant gratification was never quick enough for him. To speed things along, Bruiser emailed Emily a profane and threatening letter. He was furious the judge was prolonging their divorce proceedings. In the letter, he told Emily that she "must have pulled some stunt" to stay married to him.

Discussing her reaction to the email with me, Emily said. "Yeah, like I really wanted to stay married to a violently abusive, verbally demeaning, cheating, lying man who did not give a damn about me or my feelings." With flared nostrils, she added. "He had no respect for our marriage, none whatsoever. That never changed, not ever! Our marriage was always about him and never about us."

When Emily forwarded the threatening email to a lawyer, he wisely told her she needed to protect herself. So, she had surveillance cameras placed around her condo and recording devices installed on her phones. Once this was accomplished, the lawyer informed Emily about a private investigator he knew. He suggested she get in touch with him. Then, with s slight of smile on his face, he informed her that his firm's retainer would be $10,000.

Emily gulped. Not having any savings or being gainfully employed, once she had been abandoned by her husband, Emily's mother, with a trembling hand, reluctantly consented to write a check to retain the law firm. She secured it with equity in her condo. The attorney's strategy was to put Bruiser on the stand and make him read his intimidating email in open court.

To position Emily as a complete victim, she was told. "Don't get a job. Just sit tight."

She was directed to do this, despite the fact that she had no income and had been saddled with hefty condo and car payments. Following the advice of her attorney, a young man who seemed very competent, Emily hoped she had placed herself in good hands. Because the man was unafraid of Daren's law firm and seemed very protective, she thought things would work out well. How wrong she was.

In early December, her move from Squash was scheduled. Arriving for this, Bruiser, who had previously told Emily she could have any of the furniture she wanted, changed his mind. Predictably, his promise was a total fabrication. He also said he would pay for the movers, but this was a lie as well.

In a condo the size of theirs, there was more than enough furniture to split between them, but this wasn't good enough for Bruiser. Greedy and self-serving by nature, he took nearly everything of value, including the living room suite, the office furniture and the master bedroom suite. To make certain he obtained everything he wanted, all of the items necessary to appoint his new home with Gidget beautifully, Bruiser spent most of the day on his cell phone with her. Although she could only envision what he was confiscating, Bruiser's paramour was arranging things in her mind to furnish their place of assignation elegantly.

When Bruiser was not on the phone with Gidget, he was busy making a scene, screaming obscenities in the front yard. By the end of the day, just after Bruiser drove off with nearly everything of value, Emily looked at her barren condo. Bruiser had emptied their entire home of nearly all of the furniture, leaving her with nothing more to sleep on than an old pullout sofa bed. He didn't care. Why should he? It was all about him anyway.

When he left shortly after 11 p.m., one of the neighbors came out to complain about Bruiser yelling so many profanities all day long. The neighbor, who was too fearful to confront Bruiser personally, castigated Emily by proxy moments after her estranged husband drove off.

Being scolded for Bruiser's conduct was an additional humiliation Emily was forced to endure. If her heart had not been so devastated because of her husband's unfairness, this might have made her laugh, but it didn't. When all was said and done, all that Emily retained was her sparse office furniture, two completely empty bedrooms and a living room with two chairs, a table and lamp, and a pull-out sofa. She had one TV, the one that had been given to them by her mother. She had a few glasses but no cookware, no appliances and not even a coffee maker. Bruiser had stripped their well-appointed home to the bone.

What she retained was an abundance of memories, nearly all of them unpleasant. Their Squash home was the place where Bruiser slammed her against the living room wall, threatening her if she dared cry about it. At least she wouldn't have to worry about having a gun pointed at her again. Although this was an experience she was delighted to bequeath to Gidget, everything she had built over the course of a decade was now gone, vanished before her eyes.

This was the bad news. The good news was she still had a roof over her head, at least temporarily. Soon thereafter, her divorce decree was granted with lifetime alimony payments of $10,000 per month. She was free, alive and many miles away from the man she had once loved with all her heart. She had given up her modeling career for him and done everything in her power to make him proud of her. Instead of being a loving and appreciative husband, who had a beautiful, supportive wife, Bruiser chose to be a violent abuser instead. Perhaps this was all he was capable of being, but at least she was finally rid of him. She had survived the ordeal, thank God.

A few days after Bruiser left Squash with nearly all of their belongings, Emily received a call from her attorney telling her that her ex-husband had just filed for bankruptcy. Bruiser claimed he did not have a job other than his woodworking "hobby." Claiming impoverishment, he was countersuing Emily to stop all of his alimony payments. To fight this, the lawyer said his firm would need an additional retainer that would begin with a payment of $30,000.

Neither Emily nor her mother had access to that kind of money. Because she could not work out terms with the firm, they cut her loose. She was now completely on her own. She had monthly condo payments and a huge car payment, but no job. With Daren reneging on her "ownership" of the dealership in Jackson, which she always suspected he would do, she lacked a regular source of income.

• • •

This is how 2007 ended for Emily but 2008 would be even worse. She referred to it as "her year from Hell." As difficult as the five or six years had been that preceded it, 2008 was Emily's personal worst.

As part of her divorce settlement, Bruiser promised to pay $30,000 for renovations on her Squash condo, which were needed. Built in 1976, their home had only been repainted once. By using these funds wisely, Emily envisioned producing a lovely new place for herself, one where she could create peace and tranquility to replace the abusive shouting that had filled her days and nights for so many years. In her mind, these funds would go a long way toward achieving that goal.

Sadly, she came to realize her ex's promises were not worth the paper he had signed to make the commitment. Equally as devastating, the Great Recession of 2008 hit, and it hit her hard. Real estate values crashed as did the potential for her to find employment. Having been forced to refinance her condo at the top of its market value, Emily was unable to sustain her equity position. Broke and unable to maintain payments, she was forced to put her condo on the market. Unfortunately, all she could hope to achieve was a quick short sale.

When she presented an offer to the bank, it was refused. Because it was, she was out of options. All she could do was wait for the bank to foreclose, which was inevitable. While waiting for the shoe to drop, she was simultaneously grieving the failure of her marriage.

Even though she was better off without Bruiser, ending a marriage is emotionally difficult. Even a terrible marriage like hers is difficult to terminate, especially when it's a person's first. Divorce crushes hope.

Unlike nearly every other divorcée, Emily had an added measure of consternation. For her, the glass would never be half full. It would always be close to empty, not because she was a depressive woman by nature but because of her unique situation. Although she continued to be beautiful, she felt certain she would never be in another relationship, at least not one that was intimate. There would never be another special man in her future. That ship had sailed.

Because of the humiliating injuries inflicted by Bruiser, when he cut her vagina open with a broken bottle, he left her with grotesque scars and significant nerve damage. When she looked at herself in the mirror, all she could see was disfigurement. Because she was repulsed by what she saw, she assumed that this would be what a potential mate would see as well. Being sewn up improperly on Saint Thomas years earlier, she had ongoing medical issues from her attack.

Her injuries were the reason why Emily developed and maintained an inflexible three-date rule. After the third date, in order to avoid even the possibility of becoming intimate, she would simply disappear, leaving her potential suitors confused and bewildered. She did this out of self-protection and an overwhelming fear of rejection.

That night on Saint Thomas, in his drunken rage, Bruiser cut far more than Emily's vagina. He also carved out a piece of her soul, leaving her with a lifetime of emotional scars that would never heal. They couldn't. Like Fantine in Les Misérables, Emily knew there were "storms we cannot weather."

For her to allow herself to become vulnerable again, for her to expose herself to another man, for her to become truly intimate would never again be a realistic consideration. Her three-date rule was self-protective, but there was a hefty price to be paid for maintaining it. It left her alone, lonely and destitute, when this was the last thing she really desired. It ensured she would live a life of isolation rather than be social, which was her natural inclination. By vanishing after the third date, she left numerous men perplexed, but this was just the way it had to be. The confusion it produced was unavoidable, but it was what she required to maintain her sense of privacy and self-worth. Nothing less would suffice.

That night on Saint Thomas, when Bruiser nearly allowed his wife to bleed to death, he had no idea he also wounded her soul. He left her to bleed emotionally with a scar that would last for a lifetime. If he had realized what he had done and the victory he had achieved, there's no doubt it would have pleased him. It would have provided succor for his twisted, depraved, narcissistic soul. After all, his marriage, as well as his divorce, was all about him.

• • •

Broke, jobless and without any solid prospects for the future, Emily spent that cold winter trying to forget the man who had stolen her heart, the man who would eventually cut her to pieces, only stopping when he feared she would die.

Reconciling the difference between these two completely different people, both of whom were her husband, was difficult. Even after their divorce, this dichotomy continued to perplex her. She has never been able to resolve the confusion it produced within her. She couldn't come to terms with how two completely opposite personalities could simultaneously exist in one human being, but they did.

One thing she did know was her ex-husband was never the same once Daren Magnus entered his life. From that precise moment forward, nothing would ever be the same for Bruiser's and Emily's relationship. With Daren came money, adventure and intrigue, but he also brought an unprecedented measure of evil. Bruiser embraced Daren's iniquitous lifestyle wholeheartedly. Emily never could. Bruiser gravitated to vice like he was created to be depraved. Perhaps he was. Emily certainly wasn't.

In his deposition for their divorce, Bruiser revealed that Daren was paying for all of his legal expenses. Emily was left to fend for herself. Since she couldn't afford to keep her firm on retainer, she was referred to another attorney, a man who supposedly had a good name and a solid reputation.

The man's name was Barry Pettifogger. Although Emily had never met him, he was destined to become someone she would grow to detest nearly as much as she did her ex-husband. Semi-retired, Barry's retainer was paid by another withdrawal from her mother's home equity line of credit. There was no alternative. It was a necessary sacrifice her mother agreed to make.

Barry was a fat, oily older man who dyed his hair jet black, thinking it made him appear much younger. It didn't. Although he was incapable of realizing it, as vain as he was, this harsh dye-job made him look ridiculous, perhaps even a little clownish.

He had no manners and little concern for others or their opinions, much less their feelings. To Emily, he seemed like a carbon copy of Jud, the man who had grabbed her and, in the guise of giving her a birthday hug, dry-humped her right in front of her uncaring husband. Pettifogger was equally obnoxious.

Because no other lawyer would take her case, she was forced to use the services of this odious creature. If her divorce taught her anything, it was the real meaning of the "Golden Rule." The person with the gold rules.

By the time Pettifogger took charge of Emily's litigation, Bruiser, Gidget Midget and Emily's furniture had moved once again. They had relocated to Grand Junction, Tennessee. As it turned out, moving was part of Daren's and Bruiser's strategic plan to stiff Emily. Having filed for bankruptcy, Bruiser's goal was to avoid paying federal taxes and his required monthly alimony payments.

Beginning in February, 2008, by court order Bruiser had been required to pay Emily $10,000 per month, but he never intended to abide by his commitment. Bruiser being Bruiser, he did as he pleased, nothing more . . . nothing less. He would pay whatever he felt like, whenever he felt like it. This was just the way it was going to be. That Emily needed her alimony to pay for her mortgage, BMW payment and other necessities was unimportant, at least to her ex-husband.

To force him to honor his obligations, Pettifogger subpoenaed Bruiser's bank records. Once he received them, Pettifogger informed Emily that, because she was so poor, she would have to act as her own paralegal and go through each and every record herself. Based on what she was capable of paying, which wasn't nearly enough, Pettifogger neither had the time nor the inclination to take a look at them himself.

Understanding that her future depended on what she discovered, Emily accepted the challenge and went straight to work, performing a thorough deep dive into Bruiser's finances. When she did, she uncovered a great deal. Her ex-husband claimed he made only $55,000 per year as the general manager of the Harley dealership in Jackson, Tennessee. He was also the general manager at the Cocke County Harley dealership, but apparently he volunteered for that job. He received no compensation for it whatsoever.

At the same time, it was learned that Gidget's salary as the dealership's sales manager was $250,000 per year. Clearly, this was an attempt to divert funds from him to his mistress to avoid paying alimony, but the diversion also perpetrated fraud on the court. When asked about why Gidget's salary would exceed that of the GM's by such a large amount, Bruiser became very serious. Under oath, he replied. "It's because she has a lot of debt, so I paid her more."

When the room full of lawyers and paralegals heard this, as preposterous as his answer sounded, nobody spoke for a long moment. The room actually fell silent. Everybody present was stunned that Bruiser would provide such an idiotic and untruthful answer in a sworn deposition.

Later in the deposition, when asked why he would purchase a Cartier watch worth $300,000 while maintaining that he couldn't pay his court ordered alimony, Bruiser responded. "Well, a man's watch costs more than a woman's watch. Besides, mine has a sapphire winder." Hearing this ludicrous response, the roomful of people actually burst into laughter.

Another month when he missed paying his alimony, Emily discovered Bruiser had spent $7,500 on shrubbery to encircle his swimming pool. When he missed another month's payment, she discovered he had spent $12,000 for a Harley engine upgrade. The list went on and on. Bruiser didn't pay his court-ordered alimony simply because he didn't want to. He felt no compulsion to honor the terms of his divorce.

When asked about Daren's "business interests" in Saint Thomas and what part he had in them, Bruiser clammed up. He didn't have anything to say. When asked, "What was Daren doing in Saint Thomas?" Bruiser replied, "He had a restaurant, an estate, and was looking to buy an island like one of his buddies had done."

Emily knew that "one of his buddies" was a reference to Jeffrey Epstein, but that name hadn't become infamous at the time. The flamboyant pedophile had not yet become the famous person he was destined to be, once he was arrested in the spring of 2019.

At the deposition, Emily's attorney pressed Bruiser. "What business does Harley Davidson or Always Perfect Prime have in the U.S. Virgin Islands?"

"I cannot answer that," Bruiser responded.

The questioning continued. "Mr. Chambers, why would Daren Magnus pay for your attorney fees?"

No answer.

"What were your duties on Saint Thomas?"

Again, no response.

Any question that dealt with Daren Magnus, Bruiser either refused to answer or he simply remained silent. He did this even under the threat of being held in contempt, when the case would eventually go to court.

When the case was heard, questions about Daren were completely off limits. Bruiser protected Daren fiercely, despite potentially hurting himself by doing so.

In disgust at Bruiser's unwillingness to be candid, the judge asked. "Mr. Chambers, don't you think Daren Magnus has too much control over your life?"

Offended by such a ludicrous insinuation, Bruiser flatly replied. "No."

Shortly after this, the hearing ended. Standing up, Bruiser glared at Emily with hateful eyes. Recognizing this look, including his eyes turning black, Emily quaked with fear.

Bending down to speak, Bruiser said. "I have just started kicking you to the curb. I am going to crush you until your grandparents feel it."

The court reporter heard Bruiser say this and so did the judge. Even Pettifogger heard the comment but nothing was ever said or done about Bruiser's threat. Like so many other things, Bruiser simply got away with being a bully.

In August of that year, another hearing was held to address Bruiser's nonpayment of alimony. By this point, he owed Emily $80,000, which the court immediately reduced to $40,000, without providing Emily with any justification or explanation about why the cut had been made. Despite his major economic victory, Bruiser became so confrontational, defiant and flippant that the judge ordered him to be arrested and incarcerated.

As the Judge was leaving the bench, after having made his ruling, he said. "Let's see if Daren Magnus can come to your rescue now."

Infuriated, Bruiser began a physical altercation with one of the sheriff's deputies. As big, strong and mean as Bruiser was, his strength rivaled that of several men. It required three deputies to take him down, shackle him and lead him off to detention.

A month later, the judge held a hearing about releasing Bruiser. By this time, Daren had retained a new attorney for Bruiser, a seasoned litigator. This man actually attended the same synagogue as Emily.

To defend her interests, Pettifogger's lawyering skills were expensive but utterly worthless.

For Bruiser to be released, he was required to consult with his attorney and Emily's, but she was blocked from attending the meeting by both her attorney and Bruiser's. Without her input or permission, they renegotiated Emily's future. She had absolutely no say in the matter.

Later, as Emily thought about what happened, she became convinced Daren had "influenced" her lawyer to throw her case. Whether this was true or not will never be known. The end result, however, was catastrophic for Emily. The judge reduced her alimony by 90 percent. This meant she went from a marital lifestyle that had once been close to $60,000 per month to having just $1,000 a month to live on. Instead of the $10,000 per month Bruiser had originally agreed to pay, he was now only required to pay $1,000.

Emily was devastated. She wouldn't even have enough to maintain her health insurance. Bruiser said he would crush her and kick her to the curb. With the help of Daren Magnus, his lawyer and hers, this is exactly what he did.

CHAPTER 14

Dead in Twenty Minutes

FRIDAY JULY 19, 2019

Where privacy was concerned, Emily Chambers was all-pro at keeping secrets. Although I had known her for nearly a dozen years, after listening to her tragic tale, a story where she had experienced substantially more than her share of heartache and grief, I was amazed that she had been able to keep things together as well as she had. At least, this was my impression.

Always maintaining her poise, at least outwardly, Emily never allowed herself to succumb to a "poor me" attitude. She always held her head high. On the outside, the side she displayed publicly, she oozed dignity. That she suffered internally was not apparent. Nevertheless, the emotional wounding she experienced became obvious to me with each detail she chose to divulge.

Obviously, Emily and Bruiser were not well suited. Despite this, because they both experienced similar early childhood travails, where neither felt loved or wanted, there was a part of them that actually connected quite well. Having been placed in numerous foster homes, where abuse seemed to be his daily portion in life, coupled with his biological parents' penchant for petty larceny, Bruiser's adult life replicated the model he learned in childhood. This certainly couldn't be used as a valid excuse for what he became, but it did go a long way toward explaining why he gravitated to evil. Being programmed into him, when he became an adult, he simply followed a predictable pattern.

For Emily, who never had the loving, stable and secure home she desired as a child, more than anything she longed for the permanency and stability that owning her own home would create. Although her childhood was not nearly as dysfunctional as Bruiser's, it certainly was an unhappy one.

Perhaps, on a subliminal level, this was why the two connected so powerfully, at least in the beginning. Their connection was almost primeval. It was so physically strong that it altered the course of each of their lives irreversibly. Being magnetic, it produced energy, but the energy it created certainly wasn't the type necessary to nurture and sustain a healthy marriage. In fact, it proved to be the exact opposite.

Neither had adequate healthy modeling, especially where interpersonal communications were concerned, to replicate a normal male-female relationship. Emily's marital modeling was limited while Bruiser's was virtually nonexistent. Sadly, his marriage skills were so deficient that he would repeatedly ask Emily why she wouldn't be "more submissive, like other wives and girlfriends?"

Bruiser had no idea what women were really like and, when he learned, he didn't like what he discovered. In Bruiser's simplistic world, what he wanted was a woman who would do exactly what he wanted when he wanted it, never challenging him or even asking unpleasant questions. That he believed such women existed in the United States was a testimony to what a relational simpleton he was.

Although Emily was very attractive, which Bruiser liked, she definitely had a mind of her own, which he definitely didn't like. Despite trying repeatedly to be what her husband wanted her to be, her best efforts were never good enough to please him.

At her core, Emily was a principled Jewish woman. Because of the values that came with her worldview, she was never at peace with her husband's criminal behavior. Since she had a clearly defined, well-develop belief system that was founded on the Ten Commandments, she was never able to embrace his deviancy. To live in perpetual conflict with her fundamental beliefs was morally repugnant to her. Because it created unacceptable cognitive dissonance, she rebelled against the lifestyle her husband welcomed.

She could no more subordinate her sense of right and wrong to her husband's or Daren Magnus's twisted desires than she could participate in their sordid, depraved and violent bacchanalia. Recognizing this was probably why Bruiser and Daren excluded her from all of the boat parties.

It simply wasn't possible for her to be what her husband or Daren wanted her to be. Her values wouldn't permit it.

Bruiser, on the other hand, having no estimable or redeemable core values, had no difficulty becoming the person Daren wanted him to be. In fact, Emily's husband jumped at the chance to be a "Crotch Cannibal." Being amoral, he willingly submitted to whatever evil suited Daren's fancy.

Perhaps it was this fundamental difference between Emily's and Bruiser's sense of right and wrong that doomed their marriage. Although she tolerated her husband's depravity, enjoying the financial comfort that working for Daren generated, she never accepted the degeneracy that accompanied it. The difference between their conflicting values was unsustainable. It doomed their marital relationship. It's as simple as this.

• • •

Having learned what transpired at Estate Viol, Fisherman's North Drop restaurant and on the high seas on Daren Magnus's boat, where underage girls were sexually exploited, I wrote about the sex trafficking operation Magnus was maintaining on Saint Thomas. Once I finished, having also written about the back story concerning what occurred between Bruiser and Emily before they became involved with Daren Magnus, I felt certain I had described Emily's experiences accurately.

I wanted to present a clear picture about why Emily ended up being in the desperate situation she was forced to face. This was not certainly the life she wanted, but it was the one she had for many years.

While putting the finishing touches on this part of *The Three Commas Club*, on July 19, 2019, I began to experience severe heartburn. It started late in the morning and became progressively worse. Because I also felt some chest pain, I assumed it was acid reflux. While driving to the YMCA for my daily workout, I felt a little nauseous, so I decided not to lift weights. Instead, turning around, I drove home and took a Pepcid Complete. Fully confident this would remedy the problem, I thought my heartburn and chest pain would subside quickly, just like it always had, but it didn't.

I continued to write for a while longer, but the pain didn't go away. It intensified. By late afternoon, my heartburn and chest pain had become quite severe. I was also experiencing mild nausea. Finally becoming moderately alarmed, I called my daughter, Jordan.

Although she had her cell phone muted while feeding her one-year-old daughter, her husband saw the name "Dad" on her iPhone. Turning to his wife, he asked if she wanted to answer the call.

Nodding that she did, Jordan picked up the phone and said cheerfully, "Hi, Dad."

Replying, I said. "Jordan, I don't think there's anything wrong, but I have been experiencing heartburn and chest pains for several hours. Both are getting worse. I think it's acid reflux, but I'm not sure."

Immediately alarmed, Jordan became assertive. "Dad, you only have one question to answer. Do you want me to call an ambulance, or do you want me to come get you?"

Startled by her decisiveness, I allowed myself to be checked by her question. This was rare for me, but I did recognize the potential seriousness of my situation.

Instead of minimizing what was happening, I simply said. "Can you come get me?"

"Yes, I'll leave right now."

With her husband taking over the feeding the baby, Jordan promptly headed out. Since she lived in Franklin and my apartment was in Belle Meade, the traffic should have been horrendous on Friday night at 6:30 p.m., but it wasn't. Surprisingly, the traffic was light, which meant she arrived at my apartment in record time. When she walked through the front door, she immediately noticed my color was ashen gray.

Leading me to her car, she drove me to Vanderbilt Hospital's Emergency Room, which was not that far away. It took just a few minutes to get there. Valet parking was available at the hospital.

Walking in quickly, I addressed the triage nurse. "I'm not sure what's wrong with me. I don't think it's serious, but I am having chest pains."

By stating this and only this, I was placed at the head of the line in the packed waiting room. Vanderbilt, by the way, is one of the largest hospitals in the South.

In less than two minutes, I was taken to a room where my blood was drawn, blood pressure taken, and an EKG administered. Within a few minutes, with my troponin levels being highly elevated, I was informed that I was having "an episode." When I asked what an episode was, the emergency room physician told me that I was having a heart attack.

"I don't think so," I responded in a way that is typical of many American males. Denying reality, responding in a cavalier way to the seriousness of my situation, I added. "Besides, there has never been any history of heart problems in my family."

"Well, there is now," the emergency room physician corrected without equivocation.

Fully aware of how serious my situation was, Jordan began to ask numerous questions. Upon hearing precisely how grave my condition was, she excused herself for a brief moment to call her husband and her sister. Informing both about what was happening, Jordan told them they needed to come to the hospital immediately.

To help, my ex-wife, Martha, dropped everything and graciously offered to take care of the baby so that Jordan's husband could hurry down to the hospital where Jordan had requested his presence.

While all of this was transpiring, the hospital staff continued to perform tests. Explaining the nature of my problem, one of the ER doctors said. "Your right carotid artery is blocked. When the cardio-vascular surgeon arrives, he will put a stent in your heart."

Finally realizing the severity of my situation, I said. "Well, I hope he gets here soon."

"He will. There is a specified number of minutes for him to arrive. It's required," the ER physician explained.

By this time, my daughter Victoria and Jordan's husband arrived, but my condition was becoming more severe by the minute. With no warning, I suddenly turned from being gray to almost porcelain white. Immediately thereafter, I became violently ill, throwing up violently.

When this happened, Jordan heard the intercom nurse announce. "Code STEMI, room 14." That was my room.

Within ten-to-fifteen seconds, the room filled with people. Each worked quickly and methodically. It looked like pandemonium but was well-orchestrated chaos. Everything had a purpose—to save my life. Sedatives and morphine were administered intravenously. These drugs stabilized me quite a bit but, by this time, my color was completely gone. To Jordan, I look cadaverous. She felt certain this would be the last time she saw her dad alive.

As I was being wheeled out of room 14 to surgery a minute later, the last thing I said to Jordan and Victoria, other than I loved them was this:

"If I don't make it, tell Bren I didn't do that to her."

Both Jordan and Victoria knew exactly what this meant, so do all those who have read my memoir, *Hi, My Name Is Jack*.

Between my room and surgery, I was left alone in the corridor for a long moment. While I was lying on my back, I had time to reflect.

Tearfully, I prayed, "Lord, if this is my time, I'm ready to go."

I meant what I prayed. Because I did, a peace came over me instantly. It's what Christians refer to as the peace that passes all understanding. Because of the serenity I immediately experienced, I became content with the outcome, regardless of what it happened to be.

A moment later, as I was becoming drowsy from the anesthesia, I was wheeled into surgery where my doctors were waiting.

Once the surgery began, the doctors entered my body through the femoral artery in my groin. Then, they snaked their way up to my heart with the stent that was intended to save my life. Talking to each other the entire time, in my drowsy state, I could hear them speak, but I didn't pay attention to what they were saying. I couldn't. I wasn't that lucid.

A while later, the primary surgeon spoke loudly and sharply. "John, can you hear me?"

Although my given name is John, I've never used it. So, I responded. "Everybody calls me Jack."

Surprised by my response, both doctors laughed. Then, one of them asked. "At this point, does that really matter?"

Answering, I said. "Well, I wrote a book about my life. It's called, *Hi, My Name Is Jack*." I was actually able to say this, despite all of the tropinal and morphine present in my blood stream. Again, both doctors laughed. Although I may have been on my deathbed, I wasn't about to miss a good marketing opportunity. Authors like me are like that.

A few minutes later, the primary surgeon asked. "Can you see the monitor beside your head?"

"Yes," I replied weakly.

"Where I am pointing right now shows where your problem is. Your right coronary artery has a 100 percent occlusion. No blood is getting through. If you hadn't come in when you did, you would have been dead within twenty minutes."

Twenty minutes, I thought. Although only moderately lucid, this surprised me. Never having had a near-death experience before, never even having been in the hospital before for anything of consequence, I had a difficult time conceptualizing just how close to death I had come. While thinking about this, I fell into a deep sleep as his doctors continued to work diligently. Being told how close to death I had come was the last thing I remembered.

• • •

When I awoke, the pain in my chest was gone and it never returned. The difference in how I felt was dramatic. As I was being wheeled into the recovery room, where Jordan and Victoria were waiting, after the stent had been inserted into my heart, the first thing my daughters noticed was my color had returned to normal. More than any other factor, this assured them that the procedure had been successful. Their father would live.

Spending the night in CCU, as the medication began to work its way out of my system, I couldn't believe how close to death I had actually come. The entire experience was surreal but also very sobering. The medical team at Vanderbilt Hospital had done their work professionally and masterfully. In fact, everything during my two-day hospitalization was a wonderful, healing experience, but it was certainly nothing I would ever want to replicate.

Two days later, I was discharged with an excellent prognosis. Essentially, I was told, "There's the world, go get it."

Not needing to be told twice, I redoubled my commitment to make certain each and every day from that moment forward counted. This included doing everything I could to obtain justice for the missing underage girls who had been trafficked by Daren Magnus and his pedophile friends. This was a commitment that would soon be put to the test.

Over the course of the next few weeks and months, in addition to losing about fifty pounds of unnecessary weight—the equivalent of a little more than three bowling balls—my outlook on life changed appreciably. Although my Judeo-Christian value system was strong and had been for decades, my near-death experience changed me substantially.

My desire to serve, to do things what would really count, increased dramatically, while fretting about my daily wellbeing atrophied proportionally. Deep resolve replaced things that had previously been petty, inconsequential and frivolous.

I didn't become more religious or anything like that, but there was a substantial change within me. My God consciousness, which has always been there, increased. Instead of being diminished and weakened by my heart attack, it had the exact opposite effect. It empowered me, enhancing my sense of determination. I have heard others tell of similar experiences, but it never really meant that much to me—not until I had the experience myself.

Having a new lease on life, I made an internal commitment not to squander it.

CHAPTER 15

Terrifying People

LATE SUMMER 2019

My recovery period from the near-fatal blockage in my right carotid artery was virtually nonexistent. In nearly every way, other than fear that I might have a second episode, my life returned to normal almost immediately, except for my diet.

To avoid a second heart attack, I was told to lose weight—a substantial amount. Like millions of Americans, my diet was conducive to developing heart disease. To counteract the problem, I was told to adhere religiously to the Mediterranean diet, which I did immediately. Taking to it like my life depended on it, which it did, I lost fifty pounds in the first six months. I felt better, looked better and my clothes fit me much better. All of this definitely pleased me.

Having been sidelined from writing for more than a month because of my episode, I was thrilled to return to my normal routine, but this didn't last long. Events beyond my control checked my progress on *The Three Commas Club*.

On August 10, 2019, Jeffrey Epstein was found dead of an apparent suicide in his cell in the Metropolitan Correctional Center in New York

City. This was just the second suicide in the facility's forty-four-year history. Since Epstein was the most notorious prisoner in the federal prison system, his death became headline news throughout the United States and most of the world.

Nearly every American had an opinion about what happened. For Attorney General William Barr, the apparent suicide was so unacceptable and infuriating he tasked the FBI and the office of the Inspector General with investigating what went wrong. Like so many other politically-charged investigations, however, nothing ever came from it.

Several months later, forensic pathologist Michael Baden, who was present when Epstein's body was autopsied, said that because three bones in the victim's neck were broken, he suspected the pedophile's death was more consistent with being strangled than from suicide by hanging.

It seemed that half of the country believed Epstein took his own life, as the medical examiner ruled, while the other half were convinced Epstein had been murdered. Although this was just an interesting news item for most and an intriguing conspiracy item for a few, the impact of Epstein's death was far greater on Emily than it had been on nearly anybody else.

She was convinced Epstein had been murdered. Even worse, his demise was a clear indication to her that people like the "whales" who frequented Fisherman's North Drop restaurant on Saint Thomas had the ability to reach into the federal prison system and kill a high-profile inmate like Epstein.

That Epstein had been murdered, just to keep him from revealing the identity of those who participated in his perverted lifestyle, had a terrifying impact on Emily. If they could get to Epstein, they certainly could get to her.

Epstein's cellmate had been inexplicably moved to another cell, leaving the pedophile alone and vulnerable. Both video cameras outside Epstein's cell in the hallway malfunctioned. Plus, both guards mysteriously fell asleep on the job at the same time. Based on these factors, foul play seemed obvious to Emily.

These "coincidences" convinced Emily that Epstein had been murdered. She was certain of this despite the official finding by the medical examiner that Epstein had committed suicide. Emily refused to believe it was suicide.

I agreed with her. I didn't think it was either. The contradictions and inconsistencies were simply too implausible. We were both convinced Epstein had been murdered, just to keep him quiet. Based on our inside knowledge of how members of the Three Commas Club operated, no other explanation seemed reasonable, especially since people as powerful as the Clintons and a member of the British Royal family were allegedly involved.

That Epstein came to such a gruesome end bothered me, but it did far more than that to Emily. It terrified her. Because she had been beaten and tortured, her courageous desire to come forward evaporated almost immediately upon learning about how Epstein died.

Seeing what happened to "the gray-haired dude," plus realizing that those who were responsible for his demise would likely never face any consequences for killing him, her desire to seek justice for the missing hostesses took a back seat to her desire for survival. She became certain the same gruesome outcome would be hers.

As a result, her willingness to go to the FBI to expose Daren Magnus, her ex-husband and others abruptly ceased. Having become convinced the Bureau was untrustworthy, perhaps even complicit in Epstein's death, she changed her mind about meeting with them. She adamantly refused to come forward.

Obstinately conveying her position to me, she emailed me. "PLEASE DO NOT GO TO THE FBI." She wrote this in capital letters, adding, "This is dangerous. Very much so. And there are many ways Daren can hurt both of us. He would not hesitate to do so either. For fun!"

Receiving this email, I pushed back immediately, telling Emily we needed to stick to our original plan.

Replying, she wrote. "I do not think we should speak to them." She thought we needed to be better protected than what the FBI was capable of doing. Her alternative idea was for the book I was writing to be made into a fictional novel based on actual events. "Sort of historical fiction," she suggested. She added that I should put in the disclaimer, "some events are true but the characters are fictional." She also wanted to change the book from real time but didn't explain her rationale for desiring this.

In addition to the physical danger she was certain the two of us faced, Emily stated another concern. "We are in danger of being sued into the ground and/or killed. The Magnus's are terrifying people." Pushing her new viewpoint hard, she added. "I have the right to change my mind regarding the FBI. You should seriously rethink it too. Very seriously."

With her change in position, especially becoming dead set against confiding with the FBI, which had jurisdiction over what happened on Saint Thomas, my heart sank. I couldn't fault her for feeling the way she did though. How could I?

After having heard her story and written about it, knowing she had been the victim of so much physical, financial and emotional abuse, including being nearly tortured to death, I understood exactly why she had become so fearful and reluctant. It was completely understandable, maybe even justifiable.

Despite this, if she was unwilling to come forward as we had originally planned, the events on Saint Thomas would never be exposed to the light of day. The fate of the missing hostesses would remain concealed and never avenged. There would be no accountability for the crimes that had been committed.

Even worse, the continued actions of Daren Magnus, Bruiser and their accomplices would never be investigated. Who knows how many more girls have been raped in the years that followed the sex trafficking at Estate Viol. Because Magnus's homes in Franklin and Las Vegas were decorated to suit the desires of pedophiles, it seemed obvious he was continuing his pattern of behavior.

Although neither Emily nor I knew what Daren and his whaler buddies were currently doing, not for certain, since they were still free and affluent, what would stop them from continuing to pursue their perverted, deviant behavior? The answer was simple: nothing.

Therefore, I had to assume these evil miscreants were still involved in sex trafficking, perhaps murder as well. No other conclusion seemed plausible. Pedophiles don't change; they never change. Their depravity is irreversible.

Consequently, remaining silent, allowing the potential for other young women to be victims of Daren Magnus, was simply not an option, at least not for me. To remain quiet when I had legitimate information about this criminal enterprise wasn't something I was willing to do. I couldn't. To do so wasn't even a consideration.

In my mind, I repeatedly thought about the quotation that has guided my actions throughout my adult life. It's from Edmund Burke, the nineteenth-century Irish Parliamentarian.

The only thing necessary for evil to triumph is for good men to do nothing.

I believe the truth of this aphorism heart and soul. Because I do, despite the obvious dangers involved, I was unwilling to drop what I was writing. I wouldn't allow these sex traffickers to continue their depraved bacchanalia without being reported. I couldn't permit this to happen—not without doing everything in my power to try to stop them.

To simply turn my back and walk away wasn't in my DNA. Despite the potential economic downside of being sued as well as the threat of physical danger, my conscience wouldn't allow me to look the other way. For me, this was my Spartacus moment and I knew it.

Besides, I had already invested many months into piecing together Emily's story. I wasn't about to abandon a job half-done. When it comes to writing books, I always finish what I start.

There was another reason as well, a very personal one. Because of a significant molestation issue that happened to my daughters decades earlier, events that occurred without my knowledge, taking down Daren Magnus and Bruiser Chambers would be my mea culpa for not being able to protect my own children decades earlier. The desire to right past wrongs by pursuing current evildoers burned deep within my soul.

Although now completely alone, being abandoned by Emily, I had no idea how to proceed. I needed the help of others, but I didn't have a clue about where to go next. Bowing my head, I asked for God's guidance, but I really didn't expect a specific answer. Praying about the situation, however, did make me feel better.

• • •

Knowing I had to start somewhere, I made a telephone call to one of my longtime friends, Sammie Scott. Sammie is a street preacher for the homeless and an extremely interesting lady. Her ministry wasn't the reason why I called her though. I contacted her because she was also a fierce advocate for young women in their struggle against sex trafficking. Having been involved in rescue operations for several years, she had already helped numerous young girls escape from bondage, escape from the ravages of being a sex slave.

Through her outreach to the disadvantaged, Rise & Shine Ministry, she has helped numerous impoverished people of color in Tennessee, but I wanted to talk to her about her experiences in rescuing underage girls from being trafficked and sexually exploited.

Agreeing to meet for dinner, we dined at the California Pizza Kitchen near Cool Springs Mall. After sharing a large roasted vegetable salad and two tasty flatbread appetizers, I addressed the specifics for our meeting.

I was impressed with Sammie and have been ever since our first meeting several years earlier. As pretty and personable as she was, Sammie was even smarter. She also had an abundance of hands-on experience with sex trafficking. After providing Sammie with the highlights of Emily's story, coupled with my dilemma about how to move forward without Emily's support, or even her involvement, Sammie had quite a bit to say.

She began by addressing the issue of Emily's fear. "It's easy to see why she is scared, but you're not afraid are you, Jack?"

"No," I responded immediately and I wasn't. Maybe I should have been, but I wasn't.

"I didn't think you would be," Sammie responded. Changing directions, she asked. "Do you think Daren Magnus is still involved in sex trafficking?"

"I don't know, not for sure. But why wouldn't he continue? He's never been caught, and having sex with underage girls is what turns him on. He also likes to hurt them."

"You're right. Why would he stop? But you're going to need more than what you have. All you've got is a lot of unsubstantiated allegations that are fifteen years old. What we really need is to get the attention of the FBI with firsthand knowledge about what he is doing now." Looking at me, she asked. "Have you been following him?"

"No, I haven't," I replied emphatically. Not expecting to be challenged about this, I replied. "I haven't even considered it." Truthfully, I was a little embarrassed about being as naïve about sleuthing as I was, especially since I have already authored eight mystery novels. I was also uncomfortable that Sammie seemed to be far more adventurous than I was, but I liked this about her. She reminded me of my fictional physician-detective, Marla-Dean Kincannon.

Not suspecting that I had been taken aback, Sammie continued. "That's the first thing I thought about. I want to find out what this guy is up to, don't you?"

"Yes, of course I do," I responded, but I was not nearly as enthusiastic about being personally involved in investigating Daren Magnus as I was in connecting Emily with the FBI. My goal was for Emily to tell her story. Sammie, on the other hand, was a fireball of energy about going after Magnus. She was ready to get started immediately. This surprised me quite a bit.

When I mentioned that Magnus lived in The Hermitage at Brentwood, a gated, secure community for the wealthiest residents of Franklin, Sammie said it wouldn't be a problem to gain entrance. I should have mentioned that Daren also had homes in Rosemary Beach and Las Vegas, but I didn't. I didn't know what Daren's home in Florida was like, but I did know his home in Vegas was an 18,000 square-foot mansion nestled picturesquely near the Red Rock Mountains.

According to Emily, it was appointed magnificently. Everything was "over the top." It even had a helipad and pool house. The main floor was decorated in desert sand colors, but the lower level was completely decorated in black and dark purples, just like his home in The Hermitage. Realizing the similarity and the purpose for it gave Emily the creeps, me too.

Returning my thoughts to my conversation with Sammie, she said. "I have some good friends in San Diego. Nearly all of them are former SEALS. They are well funded. They deal with predators like Daren Magnus and Bruiser Chambers all the time." Looking at me, she added, "Going after sex traffickers has become a big time thing. You know this, right?"

"Of course, I do," I replied, but I really didn't. When Sammie informed me about it, providing numerous details, I was amazed.

Sammie continued. "It's no longer an issue that is never acknowledged, never talked about and never pursued. Quite the contrary; it has become a very big thing. I know this for a fact. We can do something about these evil guys, Jack, and we will. Believe me, we will!"

When I heard this, I stopped feeling alone. My discomfort about moving forward evaporated. I could not have been more pleased or more encouraged.

Hugging Sammie for a long moment as we ended our meeting a short time later, I had a renewed sense of confidence, knowing I would be able to continue pursuing the goal Emily and I had started. As I drove home, I smiled. I was now doing more than just writing a book. I had become deeply involved in a real-life adventure, one that had significant personal risk attached to it but was also a noble, worthwhile endeavor.

To me, it felt like I had become a real-life participant in one of my Moon Series novels. Along with Sean and Marla-Dean Kincannon, the Nick and Nora Charles of crime detection, I was now in pursuit of villains and engaged in solving a crime.

CHAPTER 16

Apprehension about the FBI

OCTOBER 2019

Knowing numerous violent, heinous acts of evil needed to be exposed to the proper authorities was one thing. Having a detailed plan about how to move forward with a real investigation was quite another.

Although I was not quite as adamant about refusing to contact the FBI as Emily was, I was definitely tentative, especially since I had not been an actual witness to anything. I knew nothing more than what would be considered hearsay evidence. This made me skittish about contacting the Bureau.

For most of my life, I would not have been hesitant in the least. Instead, I would have been eager to contact the Bureau. Taking the bull by the horns, I would have driven to the Elm Hill Pike Office in Nashville, where the FBI offices are located. Once there, I would have simply walked in without an appointment.

Unfortunately, I was no longer comfortable doing something this bold and adventurous. I just couldn't—not as aware as I had become about the way the Bureau had been behaving in recent years. There have simply been too many instances where American citizens were targeted by the Bureau for me to feel comfortable.

In my heart, I wanted to trust the FBI, but my internal restraints outweighed my desire to divest myself of the heavy burden I was carrying. Because of this, I didn't know what to do or where to turn. Nothing felt right. Just as problematic was the realization that I didn't have a plan B, nothing that was realistic anyway. I was stuck. I had no idea about how to move forward, but I also knew I couldn't remain silent. Doing nothing certainly wasn't an option.

Then, as so often happens in life, a providential incident occurred—an event that came from completely out of the blue, changing everything.

While I was sitting in my favorite chair watching the Boston Celtics get throttled by the Philadelphia 76ers on the opening night of the 2019-20 NBA season, my phone rang. It was Amanda Hillman, a longtime friend whom I had met at the Maryland Farms YMCA many years earlier. Amanda had been my state representative in the Tennessee General Assembly for four years before deciding to run for a recent vacancy on the Tennessee Senate.

Knowing Amanda would do an outstanding job and make a great Senator, I put up a post supporting her candidacy on Facebook, tagging her that I had done so. Surprised and delighted by what I had done, especially since I had a substantial following, she called to thank me. After chit-chatting for a few minutes, Amanda asked me what was going on in my life. When she did, I seized the opportunity.

"There is something I would like to talk to you about. Do you have a few minutes?"

"Sure, what is it?" Amanda responded, genuinely interested.

As anxious as I was to obtain advice about what to do next, I became willing to disclose Emily's entire story to Amanda, making certain not to divulge the real names of any of the participants.

Having served on a sex trafficking task force while she was in the Tennessee General Assembly, Amanda was extremely knowledgeable about what was happening in the battle against this problem. She ended up being the perfect person to help me. Once she listened to my story, only interrupting for clarifying details, she put on her prosecutor's hat and asked me some penetrating questions.

"Jack, do you believe this woman? I mean, do you believe your witness is credible? Do you think she is telling the truth about this?"

"Definitely," I replied. "I'm certain of it."

"So, you don't think she would make this up just to get attention?" Amanda asked for clarification.

"No, I don't believe that would even be possible. She's not looking for attention. In fact, she doesn't want any attention at all—just the opposite. I can verify her fear is genuine. Of that, I am absolutely certain."

Satisfied with my answer, Amanda raised another issue. "Because these events happened so long ago, they will be difficult to prove. You know this, right?"

"Yes, I'm well aware," I admitted.

This led to Amanda's next question. "Do you think these men are still involved in sex trafficking?"

"I do," I replied immediately. "I have no way of knowing for sure, but what would stop them? They've never been caught. They've never even come close to getting caught. Besides, pedophiles never change."

"I agree with you about that, Jack. Pedophiles don't change. Never," Amanda flatly stated. "You said the main person comes from a prominent Tennessee family, correct?"

"Yes, he comes from an uber-wealthy family.".

"Okay, if this is the case, then I want you to go to your computer. Let's see what kind of political contributions he has made. Can you do that?" She asked.

"Sure, so you think his political contributions are important?" I queried.

"Absolutely, if he has major political connections, there may not be much appetite for investigating him," Amanda explained.

"Ugh," I replied, as my stomach turned. In my heart, I knew Amanda was right, so I checked the website thoroughly. Although Daren hadn't made any contributions, other members of his family definitely had, and they were substantial. The Magnuses obviously had numerous powerful political connections.

When I told Amanda who they were and how large the contributions were, almost talking to herself, she said. "Then, I don't think I'll refer you to the person I had in mind. I have another idea though." Having made an internal decision, she said. "Let me go for now. I'm going to make a call, but I'll get back to you. Is that okay?"

"Absolutely," I replied. "Thank you for helping."

"Of course!" She replied. "I'm as committed to chasing down guys like these as you are." With that, she hung up.

Breathing a sigh of relief, I unmuted his television to finish watching the 76ers defeat my beloved Celtics.

• • •

I didn't hear from Amanda that evening but, quite early the following morning, she called. When I answered, she was very excited.

"Jack, I have just been on the phone with Xenophon Hicks, and I briefed him about everything you told me."

"Great," I replied, having absolutely no idea who Xenophon Hicks was.

Sensing this, Amanda explained. "Xenophon is the U.S. Attorney for the Middle District of Tennessee. He's very interested in this case."

"What!" I exclaimed, nearly coming out of my seat.

"You heard me correctly. He's very interested." After a brief moment of silence, she added. "You know what his job entails, don't you?"

I didn't have a clue but I winged it. Being Irish, I'm pretty good at that. "It means he's like the district attorney, right?"

"Not quite," she explained. "He's the chief federal law enforcement officer for the Middle District of Tennessee. That includes all of Nashville, Jackson and surrounding counties. He listened to me and wants to talk to you right away."

"Wonderful," I exclaimed.

"Do you have a pen?" Amanda asked.

"Yes."

"Here's his cell number," Amanda said. Then, she proceeded to give it to me. "Call Xenophon right away. He's waiting for your call."

Not having to be told twice, I disconnected and called the U.S. Attorney immediately. While doing so, I had a brief moment to reflect. Laughing to myself, I marveled at how precisely my prayer about being given direction had been answered. Equally amazing, I hadn't even been involved in making it happen.

Having specific direction, my apprehension about contacting the FBI diminished. Because Xenophon Hicks was the U.S. Attorney, dealing with the FBI would not be a hit-or-miss proposition. I would no longer have to worry about finding a trustworthy agent. Because every FBI agent in Middle Tennessee worked for the U.S. Attorney at one level or another, Amanda Hillman's networking efforts provided me with an outstanding contact. This meant Emily and I would be in a position where potential governmental corruption would cease to be a concern.

I also felt certain Emily would be pleased that the number one law-enforcement official in Tennessee would be in her corner. He would be the first person in law enforcement to hear her story. In my mind, this would be a perfect situation to bring justice to the missing girls from years earlier. I hoped it would also provide Emily with the confidence she needed to come forward.

Dialing the number Amanda provided, the U.S. Attorney answered his cell phone on the second ring. After introducing myself, knowing how busy the U.S. Attorney must be, I refrained from engaging in any chit-chat. Instead, after taking a deep breath, I jumped right into Emily's story. I provided the U.S. Attorney with a great deal of information to supplement what Amanda had already told him.

U.S. Attorney Hicks was keenly interested in what I had to say. This was obvious because he gave me his complete attention. The two of us must have talked for at least a half an hour, maybe as long as forty-five minutes. During the conversation, U.S. Attorney Hicks asked numerous follow-up questions once I completed my initial briefing.

The first question Hicks asked me was why Emily distrusted the FBI. To me, it seemed like the U.S. Attorney was genuinely mystified.

This surprised me, but I answered. "Because she watches FOX News, that's why."

After what seemed like a long pause, the U.S. Attorney let out a hearty laugh. I did too. A moment later, Hicks asked if I thought Emily was telling the truth. I assured him that she was. Having been through Emily's story repeatedly, I had absolutely no doubt she was credible. I also told him I thought she would make an excellent witness.

A while later, Hicks asked me another pointed question. "Do you think her hesitation to come forward is because she is complicit in what happened on Saint Thomas?"

"No," I replied without hesitation. "I'm quite certain she wasn't."

"How sure are you?" the U.S. Attorney asked.

"Positive," I affirmed. "She's a very principled Jewish woman. I've witnessed a substantial amount of fear in her but no guilt—none whatsoever."

Changing his line of inquiry, Hicks said. "Since these events happened fifteen years ago, this is something that will be very difficult to prove, but I am interested. I would like for the two of you to come in for an interview. Would you be willing to do that?"

"Absolutely," I replied without hesitation, although my mouth suddenly became dry.

"Good, will you make the arrangements with her?" the U.S. Attorney asked.

"Definitely," I replied. "She can be a little difficult to get ahold of, but I'll be back in contact with you by no later than tomorrow afternoon."

"Great, that will work. Thank you for coming forward and letting me know about this."

"Thank you, sir, for hearing me out."

With that, our conversation concluded. Since it occurred early on a Thursday morning, before I even had a chance to pour my second cup of coffee, I knew I had my work cut out for me, especially since I promised to reconnect with the U.S. Attorney by Friday afternoon.

Nevertheless, I was overjoyed that the wheels of justice had finally been set in motion. I felt certain both Daren Magnus and Bruiser Chambers would soon be held to account for what they had done. It was about time these two miscreants felt the heavy hand of the law bear down on them.

CHAPTER 17

It Could Cost You Your Life

OCTOBER 2019

Convinced my prayer to be given specific direction had been answered, I couldn't have been more pleased. Once I disconnected from my conversation with the U.S. Attorney, I called Amanda to thank her for her help. Without her, I felt certain I would have continued to spin my wheels fruitlessly for quite a while longer. I knew I would have floundered. With Amanda's help, however, I had direction and knew exactly what to do next. I couldn't wait to tell Emily the great news.

Later that morning, I tried to call her, but my attempt went straight to voicemail. Leaving a message, I asked her to return my call but, when she didn't, I sent her a text message several hours later informing her about what had transpired.

Answering my text almost immediately, Emily emphatically stated that she "regretted" telling me anything, adding that to have contacted the U.S. Attorney without consulting her was a breach of our friendship.

Stunned after reading Emily's hostile response, my worst fears were confirmed. Not willing to allow things settle down, I tried to call Emily again, but my call went straight to voicemail. Hanging up rather than leaving another message, knowing that she was screening my calls, I texted Emily a second time, informing her that my conversation with Xenophon Hicks had not been planned.

I stated. "The top federal law enforcement officer in the state of Tennessee has asked us to sit down with him for an interview. When they hear what you have to say, the power position is going to flip immediately. This is good news for you."

Replying immediately, confirming that she had been unwilling to speak to me directly, Emily wrote. "We both know that agents will be sent to speak to Magnus. I am as good as dead or will wish I was dead." To make certain I knew how offended she was, Emily attacked my motives by adding, "But that would make a great story."

Clearly rebuffed, Emily's purpose was to insult me and impugn my motives for wanting to write *The Three Commas Club*. Although offended, I refused to respond in kind, knowing how counterproductive that would be.

Instead, I tried to be encouraging. "We have the U.S. Attorney on our side." Hoping Emily would realize the value of such a powerful advocate, I reasoned. "The Magnuses are no match for the power of the federal government and the FBI." In reference to Daren and Bruiser, I added. "These people have bullied you for years. Aren't you ready for that to stop?"

Apparently, she wasn't. When my attempt at encouragement didn't work, I tried another approach. "What if Daren is planning on killing two or three more girls over the holidays. Would it be okay to just let this happen, when we have information that can prevent it?"

This approach didn't work either. Nothing worked. The more I pleaded with and exhorted her, the further entrenched she became in her resolute position to remain obstinately silent.

In her defiance, she asserted. "You testify. Be a whistleblower. I regret ever disclosing anything. You say it's my supposed freedom. No, it's my death."

Not yet willing to accept her refusal to come forward, I wrote. "We need to follow through with this. You know this as well as I do."

Based on her response, apparently she didn't. "There are more than eighty victims that the reporters and attorneys have in Florida. The reporter who uncovered this story has boxes filled with victim's information. Contact one of those victims and write a book with them."

Refusing to respond to her provocation, I replied. "This is not going away."

With a red line having been drawn in the sand between the two of us, Emily asserted. "I will not testify against Magnus."

With this response, our contentious interchange ended frostily. Emily assumed her refusal to participate would end the matter, but I knew this wouldn't happen—not with the U.S. Attorney having been informed that an Epstein-type group had been operating, and probably still was, within his jurisdiction. Instead of being over, it had just begun.

The following afternoon, as I promised, I texted Xenophon Hicks, informing the U.S. Attorney that the unnamed witness would need a little more coaxing before she would be willing to come forward for an interview.

Much to my relief, the U.S. Attorney responded by simply asking me to keep him informed about what was happening. His reaction bought me a little time to work on Emily—time I desperately needed.

Once again, I found myself in a quandary. Since the genie was now out of the bottle, I knew the situation would not simply go away as Emily had hoped it would.

. . .

By the time the contentious texting between Emily and me ended, it was clear she was offended that I had moved forward without her consent. It was also obvious her fear of reprisal had become greater than her desire to unburden her conscience, despite the debilitating weight of having remained silent for so long. Although she had always been fearful, it seemed that apprehension for her personal safety had increased exponentially. Her fearfulness had become so overwhelming it rendered her incapable of dealing with the current situation from a mature position.

To me, it seemed like she was emoting, behaving like a petulant teenager. Although Emily may have believed she controlled the situation, this was an illusion. Now that the U.S. Attorney had been informed, neither she nor I would ever control the narrative again. The Genie was out of the bottle.

Although I tried to point this out to her repeatedly, she was unwilling to accept this as being real. She failed to consider the possibility that the FBI might simply take the matter into their own hands. Without warning, a pair of agents might show up at her front door and insist she answer their questions.

If that happened, which I realized was a legitimate possibility, Emily's position would no longer be that of a willing witness. If she refused to answer any of their direct questions, that might be held against her. Things could get quite ugly. I understood this but Emily refused to even consider the possibility.

After texting the U.S. Attorney, I called Sammie Scott. I asked her if she had time to sit down and talk about how I might resolve the impasse. Agreeing immediately, we met at the Starbucks in Barnes & Noble near Granny White Plaza two days later.

Once I explained in detail what had happened and the predicament I now faced, Sammie understood exactly what my situation was. Having been involved in rescuing girls from sex trafficking for several years, she had witnessed Emily's mindset in numerous other victims.

Sammie explained. "Jack, you have to understand where Emily is coming from. Most people think that women who are sex slaves are chained to a bed or kept in a locked room all the time, but that's not what happens. That's not how they are confined."

Never having thought through how enslaved girls were confined, I listened closely.

"Most of the time, they aren't locked up at all. Their imprisonment is in their minds. They become so intimidated by those who are exploiting them that they believe they have no recourse other than to submit to their captors. Being mentally and emotionally imprisoned, their intimidation is so complete they become willing to submit to their captors. They obey without deviation."

"That's incredible," I responded.

Sammie added, "I know Emily wasn't a sex slave—not in the strict sense—but her intimidation is exactly like what those teenage girls experienced. Emily has it fixated in her mind that Daren Magnus is too big, too powerful and too rich to be taken down. Not even the U.S. Attorney or the FBI can do it."

I couldn't imagine thinking this way, but I felt certain Sammie was right.

She continued. "Even after all of the years that have passed since Emily's abuse, as irrational as it might seem, they still maintain their power and control over her."

"I never thought of it like this," I admitted. What Sammie was conveying definitely resonated with me.

"In Emily's mind, she really does believe Daren Magnus is more powerful than the FBI. To her, 'Epstein's murder' proves it. If they can get to someone as powerful and famous as Epstein, they can get to her. You need to understand this, Jack. Even after fifteen years, her mind is still being influenced by this false narrative."

"I understand what you are saying," I replied. "But how can it be changed?"

"It can't," Sammie stated emphatically. "Because of what happened to her, because of the traumatic abuse she has suffered, there are aspects to the way she thinks that have been irreversibly altered."

"So, you're telling me she will never get over this? She will never get past it?"

"That's correct. She won't, not completely." Sammie pronounced.

"This means you must deal with her where she is emotionally and not where you want her to be, or where you think she should be."

I was flabbergasted. Everything Sammie had to say was new, enlightening information. Having recovered from alcoholism nearly three decades earlier, I understood how a person's mind could become compromised, but I had not connected this phenomenon with Emily's situation. Since she always appeared to be such a "together" woman, I thought she was just being stubborn. Apparently, she wasn't. The twisting of her mind must have gone much deeper than that. An entirely different explanation was involved.

Finally coming to terms with this, I made an internal commitment to deal differently with Emily. Although her position seemed irrational, to her it was legitimate. Just thinking about what Daren and Bruiser had done to terrorize Emily made me want to bring them to justice even more.

After further explanation about Emily's thought process, Sammie admonished me. "You must be kind to her all of the time and never harsh."

"I don't think I've been harsh," I protested, but Sammie raised her eyebrow, suspecting I had been. She thought this because I was so clueless about the reason behind Emily's obstinacy.

Sammie was probably right. I wasn't alone in misunderstanding the thought process of someone who had been terrorized as thoroughly as Emily. Like most people, I assumed her mind would eventually heal just like her physical bruises had, but apparently this wasn't the case. Not fully appreciating the enormity of what she had been put through, including the debilitating emotional aspects of it, I failed to comprehend what was really causing Emily's recalcitrance.

Now that I had been enlightened, I made an internal commitment to be far more patient. By understanding the damage caused by her verbal, physical and emotional abuse, I knew I needed to change my approach. At the same time, I wanted the case against Daren Magnus to move forward. As much as I wanted to help Emily, I desired justice even more. I wanted Daren Magnus and Bruiser Chambers to be held accountable.

Changing the direction in the conversation once again, Sammie made a suggestion. "Given that Emily is stuck—that her ability to be forthcoming is stymied—you're going to need to make the decisions about how to proceed."

"Do you really think so?"

"Yes, you're going to have to take the reins. She can't do it," Sammie flatly stated. "Are you prepared to move forward without her?"

"I suppose so, but I'm not sure how to do it," I admitted.

"You already have everything you need. Think about it, Jack. She's already told you everything she knows. She's done her part. Now, it's up to you." Looking at me, Sammie asked, "Are you ready for what that might entail?"

"Of course," I replied, warming up to the idea. "But I've never thought about it like this." Nevertheless, I began to accept that I would need to be the one responsible for making it happen, if justice was to be served.

Challenging me further, Sammie said. "You can't be wishy-washy about this, Jack. You need to know how dangerous this might be. Are you prepared for this?"

"I'm not afraid, if that's what you are asking."

"It's more than not being afraid. These men will do anything to hide what they have done . . . I mean anything." She continued. "For just what I've been involved in, the role that I've played in rescuing girls, I've been threatened and followed. But my participation has never been as serious as what you've described about these men. You had better think long and hard about this before you proceed any further."

"I will," I replied. What she said was definitely sobering.

Looking at me dead-seriously, she concluded. "If you do continue, it could cost you your life."

CHAPTER 18

A Herculean Task

OCTOBER 2019

During my enlightening conversation with Sammie, she suggested I make contact with a woman who had been more involved in the fight against sex trafficking than she had. The woman's name was Mazie McGiver. She ran a non-profit rescue operation.

This 501c3's mission was created to empower those who were strippers, prostitutes, porn stars or had been victims of sex trafficking. This recovery group offered educational, emotional, physical and spiritual support, helping women escape their past. The goal was to help them change their futures. Her outreach also worked to help women who were broken, providing them with avenues to escape their destructive lifestyles.

Having heard some of the details about Mazie's personal story from Sammie, I knew I wouldn't be required to spend much time explaining the seriousness of what was happening. Mazie would get it immediately. Having been involved in numerous rescue efforts over the years, she had heard and witnessed things I couldn't even imagine, things I hadn't even written about in my fictional novels.

This made the exchange between us easy, much to my relief. Because of Mazie's personal history and unique experiences, she asked penetrating and insightful questions, particularly concerning Emily's situation.

Feeling certain that Magnus's sex-trafficking operation was still operational, requiring confrontation, Mazie understood that Emily's insistence about remaining mute was nothing more than wishful avoidance. Consequently, Mazie wanted to be as protective of Emily as she possibly could. To accomplish this, Mazie suggested I speak to a lawyer friend of hers—a man whose entire practice was devoted to representing sexually exploited women. Mazie maintained that having a legal opinion from a trained professional concerning the steps I needed to take was the wisest course of action to pursue. Given the seriousness of what I was attempting to do, along with the potential downside it presented, especially for Emily, Mazie strongly encouraged me to obtain this lawyer's advice.

Agreeing with her, knowing that she had far more experience with exploited women than I had, I promised to call the lawyer.

The attorney she had in mind was Terrance Stovall. Although his office was in La Vergne, just a few miles outside of Nashville, his practice extended throughout the metropolitan area.

Making the call two days later, during the business week rather than bothering the lawyer on the weekend, I reached Terrance while he was biking in the North Carolina mountains. Graciously taking time to speak with me, it was immediately clear that making contact with him was a solid decision.

After providing Terrance with a synopsis of what Emily's experience had been, as well as what was probably still happening with Daren and Bruiser, I explained in detail what my goal was. I wanted to solicit law enforcement to take down Daren Magnus's operation. My goal was to make certain both men were held accountable for what they had done to numerous underage girls on Estate Viol years earlier.

Listening intently to what I disclosed, when it became the lawyer's turn to speak, Terrance became very direct. Emphatically, he said. "Jack, it would never be a good idea for you and Emily to sit down with the FBI for an interview without having legal representation present. It just wouldn't. Especially where Emily is concerned, being interviewed would simply make her too vulnerable."

"Vulnerable in what way?" I asked.

Terrance responded. "When you agree to be interviewed by the FBI, when you go in, you may sit down thinking they are your friends, but this isn't true. They are not your friends. They are not necessarily your enemies either, but they are definitely not looking to help you."

Continuing to be direct, he added. "They are investigators looking for a crime. This is their position. I would never agree to be interviewed by the U.S. Attorney or the FBI without having a lawyer present to represent me. I don't suggest that you do it either. It would be a mistake."

When I heard this, I realized how naïve and trusting I really was. Clearly, I had done the right thing by speaking with this lawyer. Emily and I could have walked into a meeting with the FBI, where real crimes had been committed, but not by either of us. Nevertheless, both of us might have inadvertently made ourselves vulnerable. Obviously, she was at far greater risk than I would be. Realizing this made me appreciate how cautious Emily had been. She was right. Without someone like Terrance to guide us, we might have put ourselves in needless peril by not having counsel present to protect our rights.

After further explaining the reasons why we needed representation, Terrance asked me some pointed questions.

"Jack, just how certain are you that Emily is telling the truth?" The lawyer added. "I mean, is there any chance she is the kind of woman who might make all of this up just to get attention?"

"She's completely credible, Terrance." Having been asked this question by both the U.S. Attorney and Amanda Hillman, I was no longer surprised it was being asked. I suspected there must have been quite a few people who have wasted the time of law enforcement with grandiose tales that were nothing more than the figments of their overactive imaginations. Nevertheless, I was confident Emily's story was not one of them, especially since she wanted to avoid attention at all costs.

Terrance's next question was a little more problematic. He wanted to know if Emily's reticence to be interviewed by the U.S. Attorney might be because she was guilty of being complicit in Magnus's sex trafficking operation.

I don't know why, but this question surprised me. Regardless, I assured Terrance that Emily had not been an accomplice to any criminal activity.

"How sure are you, Jack?" He pressed.

"As sure as I can be without actually being present," I responded.

"I'm asking because this will be a line of questioning the FBI and the DOJ will probe repeatedly. I can assure you they will. There's no question about it. It's also the reason why she must have representation."

"I'm not sure I'm following?"

"Think of it this way. In an interview with the FBI, they will be looking for a crime—just like I said they would. To gain leverage, they might try to implicate Emily in some way. By putting her in a corner and threatening her, essentially connecting her to Daren, they could squeeze her until they obtain what they want. Does this make sense to you?"

"Yes," I replied. It did make sense. When I heard this, I knew Emily and I would definitely need Terrance to be present when we had our interview with U.S. Attorney Hicks and the FBI. Despite having done nothing wrong, we needed representation by a skilled, professional litigator like Terrance.

"Before we finish this call," the lawyer added, "there is one more item I want to discuss. Now that you have contacted the U.S. Attorney and have had a lengthy conversation with him about Magnus's operation, it's imperative that Emily follow through and volunteer to be interviewed. There's a reason why. For her to refuse to come forward at this juncture would look like she has something to hide. That's why she must make herself available."

"I've thought about that," I admitted. "But she's terrified of reprisals. She just wants this to go away."

"I know she does, but that's not going to happen, is it?"

"No, it's not," I agreed. "She's also concerned about the power of Daren's money. She thinks he's rich enough to buy people off. She doesn't believe he will ever face justice."

"That's not going to happen, Jack," Terrance affirmed. "Magnus can't buy his way out of this. Let me assure you he can't. In the past several years, the tide has turned against these pedophiles. Everybody is against them, from skin-head NAZI's all the way to Radical Leftwing Anarchists. This is the one thing everybody agrees about—finding these guys and bringing them to justice."

Although I was not convinced Terrance was correct about this, it was comforting to hear. At least, Emily and I would have a strong foundation of support when we finally did come forward. Now, all I needed was the cooperation of the star witness. Knowing it would be in her best interest to come forward willingly and not have to be compelled to do so, I needed to convince her of this. I also realized this would be a Herculean task.

• • •

Since my last exchange had been heated and unproductive, I was definitely apprehensive about making contact with Emily again but, since Terrance Stovall was going to be available for an introductory meeting the following day in Nashville, which was much closer than La Vergne, I called to see if Emily would be willing to meet with him.

Again, my call went directly to voicemail. This didn't surprise me. Suspecting I was being screened, I emailed Emily instead of leaving her a message.

In it, I stated. "Yesterday, I spoke at length with a very sharp lawyer named Terrance Stovall. All he does is advocacy work for women who have been victimized. He has offered to help, free of charge. After telling him the highlights of your story, he said he would be willing to represent you. His main office is in La Vergne, but he is meeting with a team of five lawyers on Broadway in Music Row. He asked if we would meet him, or even with his entire team. It would be completely confidential with full attorney-client privilege."

Knowing how important this step would be to protect her, I added. "I think this is a really wise thing to do, but it is certainly up to you. If you are willing, let me know. I'll come pick you up if you like. He will be there all day, so I think we can pick the time."

Responding to my email immediately, which let me know she didn't want to speak to me personally, Emily wrote. "Please stop. I do NOT ever want to discuss or ever write, much less speak of what happened to me. What I want is for the past to go away, not to be a daily semi-public thing that I deeply regret ever disclosing."

When I received this response, my heart sank, knowing the past was not going away, nor should it. Her strategy of avoidance was unwise and untenable. It also put me in a very bad position.

Emily added. "I thought all this was behind me." She believed this until Epstein's story detailed almost perfectly what her experience had been on Saint Thomas. To defend her rationale for not coming forward, she wrote. "I don't know the names of the hostesses. Files have been deleted, but not by me, and Daren never used any name other than 'the gray-haired dude'" for Epstein." She added, "Daren also admired Epstein's plane and that he owned an island. You have been kind and well-meaning, but I regret ever disclosing anything. Some things are destined for the past. I have become quite sick reliving the violence, fear, and constant stress. It needs to stop."

When I received this email, my first response was one of irritation. Nevertheless, I remembered Sammie's admonition to always be kind knowing the horrors Emily had endured. At the same time, she was placing me in an unacceptable and untenable position.

How could I simply dismiss what I knew and not seek justice for those teens who had been sexually exploited, with at least one of them being murdered? How could she expect me to do this? And what about the others who had been raped? Worst of all, what about their future victims? How could Emily expect me to turn a blind eye to all of this?

The answer was, she couldn't. For me to simply dismiss this would make me an unwilling accomplice to what had happened. I was certainly not willing to do that. It was galling that Emily would expect me to. I would not submit myself to what she wanted. To do so was totally unacceptable.

My position had not changed. I had not deviated from what we had originally agreed to do—not one iota. She was the one who changed.

Pushing back, I replied. "What you have been through is horrific. I know that, but it's not going to go away. It can't. By meeting with this lawyer, we can control the narrative, and he definitely will protect you. If you don't like what he says, we can simply walk away, and he can never say anything to anybody. Also, he said you might have a case for civil litigation. He would be willing to represent you on contingency. Meeting with him is definitely wise. Please, let's go."

After several additional unproductive email exchanges, Emily finally wrote. "What part of 'I am not and will not testify against Daren Magnus is not getting through here? You don't care about me as a person or friend, only as a witness that could make a good story. You should have said this way before you wrote a single thing about Saint Thomas. That you wanted a book in real time. To watch me suffer and twist, doing something against my will. Feels familiar. No, I mean it and it's my final answer. How many times do I have to say it? Help you help me, right."

Receiving this nasty rebuke was deeply offensive. It made me angry, but I knew better than to respond to Emily's provocation in like manner. I recognized how unproductive that would be. Instead, I contacted the attorney and told him Emily would need more time before she would be willing to meet.

Emily may have been adamant about dropping the entire matter, but I was equally dead-set about pursuing it to its conclusion. I was committed to moving forward, come hell or high water, but I had no idea what to do next. Since it was now "out there," time was certainly not on my side either.

THE THREE COMMAS CLUB

CHAPTER 19

Trumpet the Rights of the Innocent

WINTER & SPRING 2020

The holidays came and went, as did the cold months of winter and the mild months of spring. During this long period, no progress was made. Part of the reason was my health. I had another issue. Having noticed a place on my left leg that refused to heal, I finally had it biopsied. It came back positive for Squamous skin cancer. Immediately having this growth removed, I went through a lengthy healing process but other things occurred as well.

Unannounced, COVID-19 arrived from China with all of its fears and horrors. It appeared almost immediately following my surgery, restricting the movements of nearly every Americans, including mine. This meant the possibility of investigating Daren Magnus's sex trafficking operation would not be possible for quite a while.

Throughout this extended period of sequestration, everything in the United States and most of the world came to a screeching halt. Despite my desire to proceed, the cold case involving Daren Magnus and Bruiser Chambers became even colder. With no alternative, I was forced to place my commitment to bring them to justice on the back burner.

From Emily's perspective, she probably welcomed the inactivity. During this long period, there was absolutely no contact between the two of us. As contentious as our conflicting goals had become, this was probably a good thing for both of us.

To keep from being bored, I became active with other projects. I finished writing my second book about President Trump, *Defending Trump Nation*. The first book was titled, *Creating Trump Nation*.

During this same period, I wrote a screenplay for a Christian movie, *Three days in Kokomo*. Despite being as busy as I was, I never relinquished my desire to expose Daren Magnus's crimes. My sleuthing endeavors, however, ceased for seven long months.

Then, in early June, much to my surprise Emily contacted me on Facebook Messenger. She had just watched *Filthy Rich*, Netflix's exposé about Jeffrey Epstein's sex trafficking operation. Bothered deeply by the similarities between what she saw on the documentary and what she experienced firsthand with Daren Magnus, she was flabbergasted.

According to her, *Filthy Rich* paralleled Magnus's behavior to a tee. Needing to verbalize how this made her feel, because I had been her confidant in the past, she messaged me. "If you ever doubted or questioned my veracity, just watch *Filthy Rich*." According to Emily, all that was missing from the documentary was Daren Magnus.

Surprised to hear from her but definitely pleased that she had broken her long silence, I responded immediately. "I've never doubted anything you've told me; quite the contrary."

Emily stated that she was "so profoundly upset" by some of the events in the four-part mini-series that she was incapable of putting her feelings into words. It would be too disturbing her to do.

Changing subjects, she provided some additional information by messaging me on Facebook. "Out of the blue, after our writing exchanges, my ex suddenly stopped alimony but began texting me and making trips to Nashville." She suspected Bruiser was making these trips "to assist Daren with cover stories." She implied that Bruiser and Daren had been doing everything they possibly could to hide evidence of their sex trafficking activities.

When I read this, I thought about responding that neither Daren nor Bruiser would have been able to coverup anything, if she had come forward like she should have the previous fall, but I didn't. I knew how counterproductive that would have been.

While watching *Filthy Rich*, Emily was particularly disturbed about Epstein's insatiable desire for massages. This bothered her because, once her husband became involved with Magnus, Bruiser took a fancy to getting massages too. Now, she understood the real reason why. Before working for Magnus, Bruiser had never been interested in being massaged, but this changed once he began spending time at Estate Viol. Realizing the true motivation behind the massages became deeply unsettling to Emily.

It was one more verification that Bruiser was more deeply involved in Magnus's depraved activities than she had suspected. This wasn't all that disturbed her. When the mini-series showed the inside of Jeffrey Epstein's townhouse in New York, with all of its nude paintings and sculptures, Emily realized Daren Magnus's homes in The Hermitage at Brentwood and in Las Vegas were filled with similar artifacts and paintings. It seemed like Magnus had done his best to replicate everything "the gray-haired dude" had done, perhaps going so far as to commission the same artist to paint nudes for the baron of Always Perfect Prime.

One time that spring, when Bruiser showed up in Nashville unexpectedly, he asked to meet with Emily. Not having seen her ex-husband in more than a decade, she became suspicious about his reason for the request. Being concerned about her safety, she emphatically refused. She remained firm in her refusal, despite Bruiser's insistence that they get together.

That Bruiser had been so insistent heightened her suspicions even further. She wondered why, after all the years they had been divorced, would he want to see her now? What would motivate him to even ask—not just once but repeatedly? What was his true objective?

Having come to the conclusion that Bruiser, who had excellent computer skills, had somehow intercepted her communications with me, she decided to warn me about her concerns, but she waited several months to do so. After watching the mini-series, which retriggered her apprehensions, she finally decided she needed to reconnect.

Messaging me on Facebook, she warned. "Have your computer checked by a serious IT security agency for any breaches."

Startled to receive such a message, I replied. "Do you think they have knowledge of you and me communicating?"

"Yes," Emily responded immediately. "From my ex's text messages to me, I suspect but cannot prove that Bruiser hacked my laptop."

When I read this, although it seemed implausible, I became concerned, but that's not all. Her warning also irritated and offended me.

Nevertheless, maintaining my resolve to not antagonize or alienate her, which was the last thing I wanted to do, I kept my discomfort and displeasure to myself.

Since Emily had opened the door for the first time since the previous Fall, I wanted to glean as much information from her as I possibly could. If I expressed just how vexed I was that she had put my life in danger, while simultaneously refusing to inform me about how vulnerable I was, she would have stopped communicating immediately. I knew this. That was the last thing I wanted. Instead, my desire was for her to divulge everything she knew, which she proceeded to do.

I asked if she was sure Bruiser had knowledge of our communications?

"Yes," she responded immediately, saying she believed Bruiser might have copied our email chains.

If Emily was correct, if Bruiser had intercepted out emails, then my life might be in imminent danger. Daren, as well as the other "Whales" in The Three Commas Club, would do anything within their considerable power to keep their perversions from being exposed. The probable murder of Jeffrey Epstein was evidence of just how cunning, ruthless and successful these billionaire pedophiles could be.

Because Emily had been in contact with Bruiser for several months but had waited to warn me about being exposed until she finished watching the mini-series, this revealed how deep the breach between the two of us had become. If she thought I was in the least bit of danger, which she clearly insinuated, then she had the moral responsibility to alert me immediately, but she didn't. Instead, playing a fool's game of cat and mouse by keeping pertinent information to herself.

I realized the significance of what she had done immediately. Maintaining my decision to be non-confrontational, I didn't call her out on it. Perhaps I should have. Nevertheless, her cavalier contempt for my safety created a breach in our relationship that I could not accept nor would I ever forget it. To Emily, my life and wellbeing were not nearly as important as her desire to remain silent.

Taking her self-serving disregard to heart, I admitted to myself that our commitment to each other was asymmetrical. Although I had been deeply invested in her safety, there was little reciprocity. She was not nearly as invested in me as I was in her. I felt like I was being used.

If she had been concerned about me, she would have warned me immediately, but she didn't. Instead, she remained silent for months. She did this by choice, leaving me unaware and completely defenseless.

Coming to terms with what she had done, it was impossible for me to sugarcoat or spin Emily's behavior. Right then and there, I made an internal decision that the two of us could no longer be friends. I would never trust her again. Those days were over. I didn't hate her because of what she failed to do, but I lost all of my respect for her.

I admitted to myself that we had never truly been "in this together." This simply wasn't true. It was an illusion I maintained but never would again.

From the beginning, my goal had consistently been to ensure that justice was served for Daren Magnus's victims. Her goal had always been to maintain her isolating, debilitating avoidance of coming forward, even if it cost the lives of future victims. The gap between our two conflicting positions couldn't have been wider.

This was exactly how I felt. At the same time, I wondered if my conclusions were being too harsh? Was I being unfair? Never having suffered Post-Traumatic Stress like she had, I wasn't sure, but I was certain about how vulnerable she had made me. Additionally, she was attempting to make me complicit with her by insisting that I remain silent. Adamantly refusing to come forward, she was doing her best to make sure I didn't either. Again, our positions were polar opposites.

By nature, I wasn't predisposed to being fearful; Emily was. I understood this, but I couldn't get past my need to trumpet the rights of those innocent, young female victims—the ones who had been entrapped into Magnus's web of degeneracy. What The Three Commas Club was doing triggered one of my family of origin issues, fueling my desire to expose their depravity for the world to see.

That Emily could justify remaining silent was on her, but I would not allow her failure to be forthright to impede what I intended to do. I would no longer allow her adamant obstructionism to constrain me. Those days were gone.

With all of these recriminations transpiring in my mind, unbeknownst to Emily, she messaged me again. Changing subjects slightly, she said that coinciding with Bruiser's trips to Nashville and her computer being hacked, Gidget had just received her final divorce from him.

Emily wrote. "I did not know it, but they married in 2013."

That Bruiser had married Gidget Midget also surprised me. Knowing how difficult being the wife of this violent, self-serving man was, I certainly wasn't surprised the two had parted ways.

Emily speculated that Gidget discovered what Daren and Bruiser had been doing on Saint Thomas. According to Emily, after Gidget became aware of it, she abandoned the marriage. "I think she is as terrified as me," Emily messaged.

This seemed reasonable. If Gidget had discovered the truth about what her husband and his boss had been doing, then she would have good reason to be fearful.

Emily became reflective about Bruiser's newest ex-wife. According to Emily, Gidget once "told me that she wanted my life. I told her that she did not. What a curse she has brought on herself. God help her foolishness and greed," Emily concluded.

When Bruiser and Gidget moved to Grand Junction, Tennessee, not long after Bruiser divorced Emily, the newlyweds ran the Deer River Harley Davidson dealership for Daren. They did this until he eventually sold it.

Once the dealership was no longer part of their marital partnership, according to Emily, apparently their marriage disintegrated. With their divorce being as bitter and acrimonious as Bruiser's previous marriage to Emily had been, as I thought about Gidget Midget's situation, I thought some good might come from it. As bitter as Gidget probably was, perhaps having been shafted by her ex-husband in their divorce, just like Emily had been, Bruiser's newest ex-wife would make a great corroborating witness. Perhaps she would verify everything Emily had revealed. If she was angry, or had been impoverished by the divorce, perhaps Gidget would be willing to come forward. She might even be eager to do so.

If Gidget would be willing to make a statement to the FBI or to any law enforcement agency, verifying Emily's allegations, this would go a long way toward accomplishing my goal. More than anything, I wanted to make certain that both Daren Magnus and Bruiser Chambers spent the remainder of their worthless lives behind bars.

CHAPTER 20

Back in the Game

JUNE 2020

The following morning Emily contacted me again. Knowing her as well as I did, this didn't surprise me. In fact, I suspected she might have stayed up most of the night doing her best to analyze what she thought was happening, fretting about how it might impact her. Sure enough, this is precisely what deprived her of sleep.

Her theory was Bruiser had hacked into her laptop to gain access to her emails, putting her safety at risk. In her self-protectiveness, she still wasn't willing to acknowledge this would also put my safety in jeopardy. She failed to make this logical connection, but I certainly did.

According to Emily's theory, Gidget somehow discovered what her husband had done more than a decade earlier. Perhaps by reading some of Bruiser's emails, Gidget Midget had put two-and-two together. Confronting her husband about his deviancy, he reacted predictably, which led to a physical altercation. Having had enough of her husband's brutality, Gidget called the authorities and sued for divorce. To avoid jail, according to Emily's theory, Bruiser must have been willing to accept a diversionary court-ordered program of therapy.

Emily concluded this because, when Bruiser called, he revealed that he was attending therapy once a week. This surprised her because he had never been willing to attend therapy when he was married to her. Her second reason for thinking this was Bruiser apologized for "all the trauma and pain he had caused."

This might have been nice to hear if he had not simultaneously stopped paying alimony. Since he did, his remorseful apology seemed contrived and not genuine.

Based on his subsequent divorce from Gidget and his numerous trips back to Nashville, coupled with what Emily learned by watching *Filthy Rich*, she became alarmed enough to reconnect with me. When I asked to have Bruiser's emails and text messages forwarded so that I could determine the extent of my potential exposure, Emily simply ignored my numerous requests. She didn't even bother to acknowledge that I had made the inquiry. Even though I was now at equal risk, she refused to provide me with the information I required to assess my level of vulnerability.

After a flurry of messages that June morning, she went dark again, precisely like she had seven months earlier. This didn't surprise me. I knew it would happen. Nevertheless, I refused to become discouraged or frustrated. Those days were over. I would no longer allow her fear-based behavior to influence my behavior.

Instead, I called my friend, Sammie Scott, and asked to have lunch with her again. Meeting at Mere Bulles in Brentwood a few days later, it was the first time I had dined at a restaurant since late winter, when the sequestration for COVID-19 began. Once the pandemic hit, fear of the virus closed nearly everything in Tennessee, including restaurants.

Eating out was wonderful. Taking a bite of my seared plum salmon was as satisfying as drinking a glass of cold water on a hot day in the middle of the desert. I loved every bite of it. What had once been common now seemed unique and special.

When we finished eating, I brought Sammie up to speed about what had transpired with Emily. Knowing I needed to make a move, Sammie suggested we contact a detective she knew in Rutherford County. Sammie said her friend, Detective "Spyder" Webb, might be able to help.

Having aided her frequently in efforts to rescue girls who had been sexually entrapped, Sammie had complete confidence in the detective. Having banged my head against the wall, making almost no progress for months, including when I contacted the U.S. Attorney for Middle Tennessee, I jumped at the opportunity to tell the story to a real detective.

Suspecting my safety might be compromised, I no longer had any qualms about contacting the police, despite Emily's fervent desire that I keep my mouth shut. Remaining silent might work for her, but it certainly didn't work for me. Although I needed to protect myself, there were other reasons why remaining silent wouldn't work for me.

Out of fear for her life, Emily was willing to turn a blind eye to what had happened and was probably still happening. I couldn't do this and I wouldn't allow her to entrap me into being a passive enabler to Daren's, Bruiser's and The Three Commas Club's perversions. Being the father to four girls and the grandfather to five, there was no way I would submit myself to Emily's position, regardless of the consequences.

Agreeing to Sammie's plan, I said I would make myself available for an interview whenever the detective could see us. Driving off a short time later, I felt encouraged for the first time since well before the pandemic began. I was back in the game.

• • •

Sammie contacted Detective Webb later that afternoon and a meeting was set up for a few days later. Heading to Rutherford County, which is quite a drive from Belle Meade, I met Sammie in a parking lot. Because our meeting was scheduled just a few days after the shooting of Rayshard Brooks by an Atlanta police officer at the Wendy's near the airport, tension filled the air. It could even be felt as far away as police headquarters in Rutherford County, over two hundred miles from where the shooting occurred.

I didn't know what to expect when I met Detective "Spyder" Webb, but I was definitely surprised when I did. The first thing I noticed was the detective was accompanied by a small service dog who was wearing some sort of vest. The dog was old, very friendly and had full reign of the detective's office. Half the time during the interview, the dog sat in the detective's lap. The other half, the dog spent wagging his tail next to me, trying unsuccessfully to get petted. That this might be distracting seemed to be irrelevant to the detective.

Detective Webb had a short crewcut. It resembled Jack Webb's on *Dragnet* in the 1950s TV show. Wearing chinos and a jersey, the detective had a gun strapped to his leg that was impressive, formidable and a little intimidating. Somewhat shorter than me, Officer Webb looked to be in his late forties or early fifties, but the most noticeable thing about him was he had a pinch between his cheek and gum during the entire interview. Routinely, while sitting behind his desk, he leaned over to spit into his wastepaper basket.

Each time this happened, my stomach lurched but I successfully camouflaged my desire to vomit. This aspect of my interview was difficult. It seemed like we were participants in a scene from *Dukes of Hazzard*, but we weren't. This was real.

Thankfully, the detective never seemed to recognize my revulsion. Although he yawned frequently, being the middle of the afternoon, he still listened to what I had to say. When I mentioned Daren Magnus by name, the detective's interest perked up considerably.

Spotting this, I asked. "Detective Webb, have you ever heard of Daren Magnus?"

"I sure have. I went to high school with him," Detective Webb replied, grinning broadly but making certain not to dislodge his Skoal.

"What?" I exclaimed, genuinely surprised, forgetting all about the Skoal. In a city this size, what would be the odds of this happening? They must have been infinitesimally small.

Sammie interjected. "Wow! This is confirmation we have come to the right place. Thank You, Lord."

Concurring, I followed up by asking. "When you were in high school with him, would you have ever suspected Magnus capable of sex trafficking and murder?"

Replying, Detective Webb said. "Let's just say he didn't have a good reputation back then."

As the interview progressed, Detective Webb asked. "What makes you so intent on pursuing this?"

Taking a deep breath, I replied. "Do you remember the saying, 'The only thing necessary for evil to triumph is for good men to do nothing?'"

Smiling, the detective nodded his head in affirmation, connecting with me in a powerful way. This was a dramatic moment between us. It's the way good men have of connecting about a righteous cause.

A few minutes later, the interview concluded. As Sammie and I walked to our cars, we felt good about what had transpired. What would come from it neither of us knew, but I felt confidant I had given it my best shot.

...

Predictably, an investigation being a marathon and not a sprint, nothing happened for several weeks. When I emailed Detective Webb, it took him more than a week to respond. I think he must have been on vacation.

I no longer thought about police investigations the way I once had. Unlike TV shows, they seem to take forever. During this period, I had time to reflect about why I was so determined to pursue Daren Magnus and Bruiser Chambers. When Detective Webb inquired about my motivation, it actually startled me. That I was as determined as I was seemed like a no-brainer, but it did force me think about his question.

I thought, what man who has daughters wouldn't feel this way? If you have a daughter or a granddaughter, you want the very best for them. You want them to be loved, to be cherished and to be fulfilled. They are special and deserve to be treated that way. They are not sexual toys to be exploited by powerful men who are devoid of feeling remorse or empathy. They are not objects to be used, abused and discarded by narcissistic billionaires who are so arrogant they believe they have the right to rape underage girls with impunity.

That neither Daren, Bruiser nor any of the Whales cared about what they were doing to these young girls deeply offended me. I believe they are worse than Epstein. "The gray-haired dude" robbed his victims of a meaningful life. He not only raped their bodies, but he also raped their souls, leaving them to bleed emotionally for the rest of their lives. The victims of Magnus and Chambers may have suffered an even worse fate than this. Some lost their lives as well.

Other than serial killers, I believe pedophiles are worse than murderers. Most murderers only kill one person, usually someone they know. Each pedophile destroys the life of dozens, sometimes even hundreds, like Daren Magnus has done over the years. They rob young girls, and sometimes boys, of their innocence and their youth.

Despite the impetus to normalize pedophilia, it isn't normal. It's anything but normal. Instead, it's deep perversion. It's a way of life that must be confronted and stopped by decent men and women. I cannot imagine thinking any differently. To do anything less than what I was doing wasn't acceptable. Pursuing justice for these young victims was nothing more than me being me.

This was definitely my mindset. Because it was, there was no way I could simply walk away from what had been disclosed to me. To have do so would have adversely impacted my self-worth. Consequently, each setback increased my determination to bring these evil miscreants to justice. Someone had to do it. Like Isaiah responding to God, in my heart, I said. "Here I am, send me."

To address the problem of rampant pedophilia, a crusade against it needed to be waged. To have a crusade, you must have crusaders. Having daughters and granddaughters who were victimized by pedophiles, I couldn't think of an activity more worthwhile than exposing the evildoers of The Three Commas Club.

Emily came to me. I didn't solicit being involved. She chose to confide in me because she considered me to be a man of integrity. Because I have this character quality, it is the reason why I refused to abandon my righteous cause. I had to see it through, regardless of the consequences. To do differently, even if it would bring harm upon me, wasn't an option.

While mulling over what to do next, my cell phone rang. It was late in the afternoon at the end of July. Seeing that it was Sammie, I answered immediately. She told me she had just received a call from Special Agent Sharon Scott of the FBI. Although I had no idea who this was, this surprised me quite a bit. Apparently, Detective Webb had thought enough of what I had divulged that he contacted the Bureau and asked them to pursue the matter.

Sammie came straight to the point. "The FBI wants to set up an appointment with us right away. Do you want to do this?"

"Of course, I do."

"Then, I'll set it up. When can you be available?"

Excitedly, I replied. "Whenever it's convenient. The sooner the better."

• • •

True to her word, Sammie made the appointment for the following Monday at 1 p.m. Since she lived in Rutherford County, we planned to meet at the FBI's satellite office in Jackson rather than at the Elm Hill Pike Office in downtown Nashville. At the last minute, however, because she had a pressing medical issue, Sammie couldn't attend. Since I was the one with all of the information anyway, I was determined to keep the meeting.

Arriving a few minutes early, I assumed the satellite office would be small, perhaps in a strip mall or something similar, but it wasn't. It was huge, impressive and foreboding. Sitting on top of a hill, it was surrounded by an iron fence that was nearly as impenetrable as the Southern Border Wall.

I wasn't allowed to simply walk in. There was a freestanding guardhouse protecting the main building. When I approached, the guard was standing behind a plexiglass window like a drive-through bank teller to greet me. When I stated my business, he informed me Agent Scott would have to come down to escort me into the building.

Fifteen minutes later, she arrived. By that time, standing in the midday Tennessee sun, I was sweating profusely. After having my temperature taken to screen for COVID-19, I left my cell phone at the guardhouse and was led inside the massive FBI satellite office. The atrium was huge and impressive, so was the expensive marble floor. Instead of going to her office, I was led into a small interview room off of the main entrance. Once seated, I began to be interviewed by Special Agents Sharon Scott and her partner, Special Agent Terry Burns.

Both agents were impressive, accommodating and very professional. Sharon, who was in her late thirties, was quite attractive. Her partner, also in his thirties, looked like he could have played the part of an undercover agent bringing down drug kingpins. I liked both of them.

While telling my story, Agent Burns interrupted me often to ask penetrating and insightful questions, all of which I did my best to answer. His questions let me know the two were taking Emily's story seriously. When I was challenged because the probable murder of the one hostess wasn't a federal crime, which I knew, I replied. "But taking runaway, underage girls from the Florida panhandle, driving them to Tennessee, then flying them to Saint Thomas to have sex with men in The Three Comma Club is a federal crime, isn't it?"

Both agents affirmed that federal crimes were committed if this could be proven.

Toward the end of my intense interview, Agent Scott said. "We will perform due diligence on this to determine whether or not there is enough evidence to warrant an investigation, but we will need to interview Emily. We'll let you know before we call her. You can either let her know about this or not. That's up to you."

Knowing how she would respond, I said, "Let me think about that, okay?"

Agent Scott simply nodded her head.

When the interview was complete, I retrieved my iPhone and drove off. Having finally divulged everything I knew concerning Daren Magnus, Bruiser Chambers and The Three Commas Club to the FBI, I felt a heavy burden had been lifted off of me. Feeling exhausted, I did very little for the rest of the day. I had accomplished my part.

Now, it was their turn. Would the FBI take the ball and run with it or wouldn't they? I didn't know.

• • •

Having heard nothing from the FBI for three weeks, I sent Agent Scott an email, asking if there was anything else I could do to help with their investigation.

Responding quickly, she wrote. "Hi, Jack. Nothing at this time but I appreciate you checking in."

Remembering the process resembled a long-distance race and not a sprint, I wasn't surprised. By sending her the email, I hoped to let her to know I was not about to abandon the pursuit—no way I would do that.

CHAPTER 21

A Strategic Decision

OCTOBER/NOVEMBER 2020

Having cast my lot with the FBI, I was totally dependent on their efforts. My fervent hope was for them to take what I had told them seriously and pursue an investigation vigorously. After three months of waiting, however, I still hadn't heard a word from them. They never mentioned interviewing Emily again either. That made me think they weren't pursuing it.

I began to think they hadn't taken what I told them seriously enough. I wanted them to discover linkages to other members of The Three Commas Club, where I believed they would collect a trove of supportive evidence. I wanted them to interview pertinent witnesses, especially Emily, but this never happened. Nothing seemed to happen.

I had hoped they would arrest Daren Magnus and Bruiser Chambers. If everything I desired happened, then I felt certain other arrests would follow, including the incarceration of a slew of very rich, powerful and politically-connected men—depraved individuals who chose to abandon moral restraint for a brief moment of wanton carnal pleasure.

These evil miscreants, who were only interested in their own gratification, didn't care what happened to the underage girls they raped. Nor did it bother them they were inflicting a lifetime of emotional trauma on their victims, just to get an orgasm. All they wanted was to exploit these young girls shamelessly. I doubt they ever gave any of them a second thought. Why would they? These girls were a commodity to be utilized, nothing more.

That Daren Magnus had gotten away with his sex trafficking operation for so long astonished me, but it shouldn't have, not when I realized what Jeffrey Epstein had done with impunity for several decades. Based on the information I felt certain was true, Magnus's depravity rivaled that of Epstein's. It may have even exceeded it.

Magnus's victims, some of whom are no longer with us, needed a champion. Once Emily abandoned her desire to seek justice, out of fear for her personal safety, I knew I had no choice other than to come forward with what I knew. By abandoning her original purpose, she had hung me out to dry, forcing me to come forward alone rather than be a passive enabler like she was.

Having done so, having been completely transparent and forthright with the FBI, I had left everything in their hands. When I did, I lost control. I understood this would happen, but I never even had the assurance the Bureau was proceeding with an investigation. They never confided in me about anything one way or the other.

This left me completely vulnerable, Emily too. Although this was unsettling, I might have been okay with this, knowing it was the price required for justice to be served, if several unusual things hadn't occurred.

In early October, 2020, Emily contacted me numerous times within a short period, her specialty. This time it was by Facebook Messenger. She wanted to inform me about some new developments.

The previous day, she had received a phone call from a private number. Thinking it was a deliveryman needing the code to enter her gated community, she answered. Instead of who she expected, the call came from two men who introduced themselves as producers for a local TV station. They said they were doing an expose and wanted to ask her some questions, beginning with whether or not she knew Patrick Bellinger, Daren Magnus's lawyer.

Not expecting the call and fearful about why she would be contacted in the first place, Emily was flustered. She was also a little frightened. She was so taken aback she couldn't even remember the names of the men who called her. She didn't remember the network they represented either. All she could recall was one of the men was named Bill. Obviously, this didn't narrow the field much.

Once they finished asking several questions about Bellinger, they proceeded to ask her numerous penetrating questions about Daren Magnus. Being quite specific, they narrowed their focus to his activities on Saint Thomas. To Emily, it seemed like they already knew a great deal about Magnus, including being aware of Air Daren, Viol Enterprises and Fisherman's North Drop, but they never asked any specific questions about Magnus's alleged involvement in sex trafficking or pedophilia.

As Emily and I went back and forth, texting each other about her phone call, I wondered what these two producers were really attempting to accomplish. My interest focused on who the two men were and why their cell phone number was private. Because of how startled Emily was to receive such a call, having never been contacted about Daren's business ventures for the last dozen years, she couldn't imagine why she was being contacted now. She had no knowledge about any current, pertinent or relevant information concerning what Daren Magnus was doing.

Despite this, these two men proceeded to ask her numerous questions about his activities. When the conversation was finally over, Emily kicked herself for not being more assertive. She knew she should have asked who these men were and what they were really after. She wondered if they might have been police or the FBI but dismissed this thought because law enforcement normally identifies themselves before asking questions.

About to conclude these men were who they said they were, another disturbing possibility struck her. She wondered if they could have been associated with Daren Magnus in any way. If they were, then this would mean Daren and Bruiser knew she and I had been communicating for over a year-and-a-half. If this was the case, then we were definitely vulnerable.

Perhaps Bruiser had hacked into her emails as she had feared. If this was true, then our lives were unquestionably in danger. When she began to message me about this possibility, I became concerned.

To continue covering up what they had done, "taking care" of Emily and me wouldn't phase them in the least. After all, everybody knows dead men tell no tales. To keep their deviancies from being exposed, these men would go to any extreme. To both Emily and me, the fate of Jeffrey Epstein proved this. If he could be terminated while in a maximum security jail, taking care of loose ends like us would be easy.

As we continued to text, I thought the possibility they had discovered our communications was remote, but it did exist. If they knew, the implications were truly terrifying. On this note, with nothing left to discuss, our communication stopped as quickly as it had started.

I was concerned. My first thought was whether or not the FBI had contacted Emily. Because the callers were two men and not a man and a woman, I doubted it was the Bureau, but I needed to be certain.

To get an answer, I sent an email to Special Agent Sharon Scott, recapping my communications with Emily the day before. I concluded by writing. "I thought you needed to know this. Nobody has ever contacted her before, so she's nervous."

Shortly after sending the email, Special Agent Scott responded. "Thanks for sharing this information Jack."

But this was all there was. That was her entire message, nothing more. Although being cryptic is routine for the Bureau, I wanted and needed to know more. I wanted to know whether or not Emily's life and mine were in danger, but I also knew I wouldn't receive any further information from them, not the FBI.

That I was being left in the dark was frustrating and concerning. It left me in an awkward, precarious position. Having come forward, I had been responsible for uncovering both of us. Because Emily and I were the ones who were vulnerable, not the FBI agents, I began to think of ways to lessen our exposure. Maintaining Daren's and Bruiser's secrets in a shroud of silence had been Emily's strategy to remain safe but, now that others were looking into what happened on Saint Thomas, perhaps even a television network, her position no longer seemed viable.

Since the FBI wouldn't allow me to know if they were proceeding with the investigation or not, even though Emily and I were exposed, I knew our continued safety was my responsibility. As I assessed our situation, I concluded it didn't seem to matter to the FBI whether or not we became collateral damage, but it certainly mattered to us.

We were on our own.

Although I knew I had a responsibility to come forward to champion the rights of past and future victims of The Three Commas Club, I also wanted the two of us to live to tell the tale. Emily had entrusted me with her deepest secrets before retreating to silence. This was frustrating but, in fairness, she was the one who had been beaten and impoverished. I had only written about her experience. I hadn't lived it. She witnessed what happened to the hostess the cleaners dragged off. Emily saw what happened to that girl, not me.

Her fear was real. It debilitated her. I understood this completely. It fueled my protective and survival instincts.

The final event that forced my hand was the most bizarre of all. It was totally unexpected. In Rutherford County, where Detective Spyder Webb was employed, his boss, Chief Deputy Buford Bottomly was arrested for dealing in child porn. Even worse, Bottomly had recently been elected to the Federal Bureau of Investigation's National Academy of Associates executive board. This placed him in regular contact with leadership within the Bureau, not only in Central Tennessee but throughout the Southeast. Bottomly, a pedophile, was well connected.

When Sammie Scott informed me about what had happened, I couldn't have been more surprised. My fear of being exposed by coming forward skyrocketed. This time it was from the inside, from law enforcement itself. I was furious.

When Sammie and I called Detective Webb to determine the extent of my vulnerability, the detective assured me that Bottomly, who had been taken off in handcuffs the day before, hadn't compromised my efforts. Nevertheless, I remained unconvinced. That such a possibility was now part of the equation was galling. I knew I needed to act swiftly and decisively.

Weighing my options, I made a strategic decision—one that would have life-altering implications for both Emily and me. Even though our lives hung in the balance, knowing how opposed she would be to what I intended to do, I chose to proceed without her knowledge or her blessing.

My strategy was bold but also risky. If it was successful, members of The Three Commas Club would be completely exposed for the world to see. Future victims would be spared from a lifetime of heartache and past victims would receive the justice they had been denied for years. Finally, for the first time in more than a decade, Emily would be able to live free from fear.

If it didn't work, then the outcome would have an entirely different outcome. At bare minimum, I might end up dead, perhaps from a self-inflicted gunshot wound to the head. I'm certainly not suicidal, but I had to face the possibility that this might happen. The ending to *The Three Commas Club* would have to be written by someone else. I would no longer be around to pen what happened. *Que sera sera.*

THE THREE COMMAS CLUB

CONCLUSION

The End May Just Be the Beginning

NOVEMBER 2020

If *The Three Commas Club* was a novel, this would be the time when the FBI would make a dramatic entrance. Having concluded their rigorous investigation, they would raid all three of Daren Magnus's homes, arrest him and bring him to justice—Bruiser Chambers too. Once in jail, to make the conclusion emotionally satisfying, Daren would confess to everything, implicating dozens of others.

But, this isn't a novel. It's real life and real life doesn't have tidy endings. In this situation, the story doesn't even have an ending. Having informed a local detective in Rutherford County, the Deputy U.S. Attorney for Middle Tennessee and the FBI about Magnus's sex trafficking operation, I have done everything possible to expose what Daren, Bruiser and The Three Commas Club have been doing. I have done my best, but will my efforts be enough?

I have no idea. Candidly, my gut level tells me nothing will happen. They will continue to get away with it and there will be no accountability. I hope I'm wrong.

Because I doubt that I am, I'm going to force the issue. I'm taking the situation back into my own hands. Since I'm responsible for doing everything I can to protect Emily and me from being harmed, I've made the decision to conclude this story by raising public awareness about what has happened by telling everything, keeping nothing secret.

This is why I have made the decision to self-publish *The Three Commas Club*. To increase awareness about what has happened, I will promote the book through my extensive social media network. Having written twenty-five books so far, there are a significant number of people nationwide who will read this story. I know this will happen. I'm not guessing.

Recognizing the danger I will face by exposing these degenerates, I am asking others to get involved in exposing them too. This means I am asking you.

Having read Emily's story, you have become keenly aware of the depravity of Daren Magnus's massive pedophilia and sex trafficking operation. You have seen and vicariously experienced the impact of his depraved indifference to underage girls. Because you have, I am asking you and other readers like you to help me right this wrong. Join me in this fight for the truth. Help me expose the Whales of The Three Commas Club. Help me obtain justice for these victimized teenage girls. Help me provide closure for members of their families. Help me put an end to this perverse criminal enterprise. Help me right these wrongs.

By taking *The Three Commas Club* public, by exposing these powerful evildoers to public scrutiny, I have definitely placed myself in danger. When Daren, Bruiser and the Whales realize the extent of their unmasking, they will be frightened and enraged—a perilous combination.

To stop me, one or two may attempt to silence me permanently.

The threat to me is real, not ginned up. This is why I need your help. I am appealing to your sense of justice. If you have been offended by what you have read, if righteous indignation has been stirred within your heart, then act upon it. Do more than just pray for my safety. Be active. Contact law enforcement and insist that these criminals be brought to justice. Contact your Senators, members of the House of Representatives or anybody else in a position of authority. Insist they get involved.

If you know anyone who has been the victim of sex trafficking, inform them about *The Three Commas Club*. If you know of a family who has a missing child, tell them about *The Three Commas Club*. If you know any advocacy groups for the victims of sex trafficking, tell them about *The Three Commas Club*.

The more widely known this book becomes, the safer Emily and I will become. My strategy for survival is the exact opposite of Emily's. She has chosen silence, while I intend to broadcast the truth far and wide, including interviews and speaking forums.

By reading *The Three Commas Club*, although it was not my original intent, I'm soliciting your active involvement. I need you to join me in righting this massive wrong. It is my fervent desire that you act upon your outrage to this ongoing injustice. Will you help?

The more people who read *The Three Commas Club* the better. There is strength in numbers. This is what will keep Emily and me safe.

Perhaps you know a family who hasn't heard from a runaway daughter for years. If this is the case, many of these victimized families will want to read *The Three Commas Club*. I can assure you they will demand answers. Wouldn't you, if you had a missing daughter? As a dad, I certainly would.

Daren and the other Whales are depraved men who have used their wealth to hide their depravity. They have gotten away with aberrant behavior for long enough. Their behavior simply cannot be allowed to stand. It's as wrong as wrong can be. Now, it is up to us, you and me, to put a stop to them. They must be brought to justice—the sooner the better.

By speaking out, by insisting that justice be served, we can make certain the Whales cannot buy their way out of the crimes they have committed. None of them deserve mercy, not even a smidgen of it.

By going public with *The Three Commas Club*, I am acting as a whistleblower. This is risky but so is remaining in the shadows, hoping for the best by waiting on the FBI. This is especially true after Emily was called by the two TV producers. Their call changed everything. Remaining silent ceased to be an option at that point.

By publishing *The Three Commas Club*, even though I've changed the names and places, Daren and Bruiser will recognize themselves. How could they not? Like Satan in the Last Days, they will realize their time is short. This will increase Emily's and my danger exponentially.

This is why I am appealing to you. Evil can only flourish when the righteous do nothing. By shining light into the darkness, I have exposed a pattern of evil that has thrived without consequence for far too long. This has to end. Good men and women must stand and demand justice.

As I've stated, I have changed the names and locations of those involved, but I also have written a completely accurate version of *The Three Commas Club*. That version identifies these evildoers with 100 percent accuracy—all of them. But, that's not all I've done. I have sent the accurate copy of the manuscript to a dozen people across the United States. If any harm befalls either Emily or me, the accurate version will be released immediately to law enforcement, including the FBI, and to trusted people in the publishing world. It's my fervent hope that this will ensure our safety.

The last thing either Daren or Bruiser want is to be put in the spotlight. Cockroaches never like daylight. This is our insurance policy and the specific reason why I am going public. By sitting down with Emily to hear her story a year-and-a-half ago, I never anticipated being in a position like this, but here I am.

In some ways, the end of *The Three Commas Club* may be just the beginning. As long as I have breath in my body, as long as I have the ability to write cogent sentences, I will pursue miscreants like the Whales. I will write about sex trafficking and victims of pedophilia until I die. I have to. It has become part of my DNA.

I've always believed the only thing necessary for evil to flourish is for good men to do nothing. I still believe this aphorism. It's why I continue to write. Who knows, there may even be a sequel. I'm certainly open to that.

Memoirs/True Stories by Jack Watts

Hi, my name is Jack
One Man's Story of the Tumultuous Road to Sobriety and a Changed Life
JACK WATTS

Steven Sarkela with Jack Watts
Betrayal in Charleston
Extortion, Torture and FBI Sting

THE Three Commas Club
A True Story of Sex Trafficking Pedophilia & Murder
Jack Watts

Moon Series Novels by Jack Watts

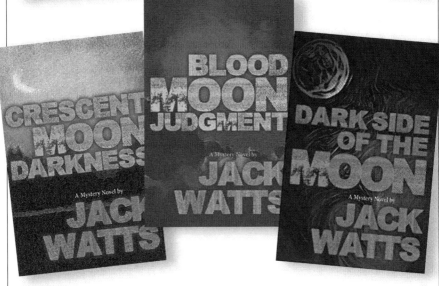

More Novels by Jack Watts

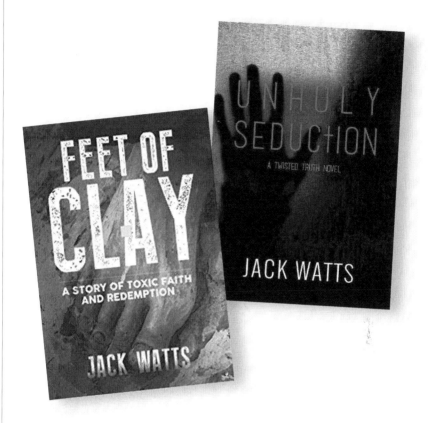

Politcal Books by Jack Watts

Made in the USA
Coppell, TX
09 March 2021